ENCOURAGING DEVOTIONS

FOR BOYS

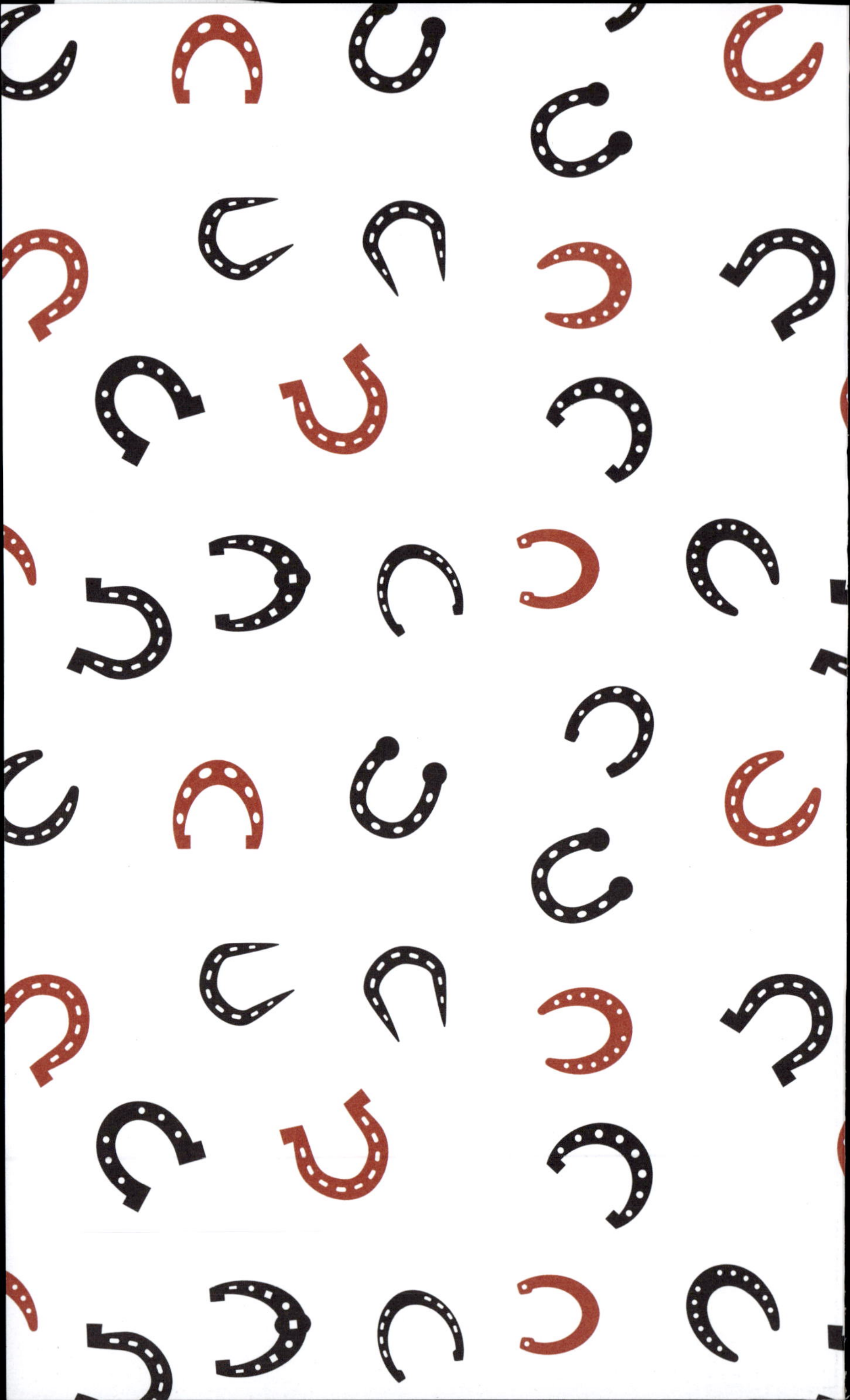

GLENN HASCALL

ENCOURAGING DEVOTIONS

FOR BOYS

180 READINGS TO GROW YOUR FAITH

BARBOUR kidz
A Division of Barbour Publishing

ISBN 979-8-89151-206-1

Published by Barbour Publishing, Inc., 1810 Barbour Drive, Uhrichsville, Ohio 44683, www.barbourbooks.com

Our mission is to inspire the world with the life-changing message of the Bible.

Member of the Evangelical Christian Publishers Association

Printed in China.

002662 1025 HA

INTRODUCTION

These devotions and prayers were created just for you!

Take a few minutes to strengthen your spirit with these inspiring devotions, scriptures, and prayers that will draw you closer to God's heart and help you discover the awesome impact of God's Word on everyday life.

Touching on topics like respect, kindness, character, loyalty, honesty, and so many more, these just-right-sized readings will meet you right where you are in life. *Encouraging Devotions for Boys* is a great way to help you grow your faith!

"I will be a Father to you. You will be My sons. . .says the All-powerful God."
2 CORINTHIANS 6:18

THE QUEST BEGINS

Listen to words about what you should do. . .
so that you may be wise the rest of your days.
PROVERBS 19:20

There are things you should know, believe, and do. Chances are pretty good that you don't know all of them. That's why reading this book can help.

The advice you'll read here started in God's heart and is shared in His Word. As you pay attention to it, you'll start to become a boy after God's own heart.

Read the words that share the heart of a God who loves you. Each day, when you open this book or turn a page, you can find God waiting to share something that takes what you know and challenges you to make decisions like He makes.

Pay attention to the verses you read and the encouragement each devotion provides. Reading these devotions is more than something to check off a to-do list; it's the beginning of a quest. Check in every day for a new assignment. Turn the page, and let the quest begin!

Give me the courage to move forward in this adventure with You, God. You have things to teach. Give me the wisdom to learn.

FAIR, KIND, HUMBLE

What does the Lord ask of you but to do what is fair and to love kindness, and to walk without pride with your God?
MICAH 6:8

★

To begin this quest, you admit you're seeking God. And when you seek Him, He promises you will find Him! Your next step is to agree that His way is good—while you seek to do what He asks.

Today's verse offers three things you can do *now* that will help you tomorrow. These three things are choices that become habits that become a new and better way to live. Ready? . . .

Play fair. Be kind. Humbly follow God.

Play fair. Refuse to cheat. Include others. Don't make friends with people because of what they can do for you.

Be kind. Go out of your way to help people. Don't be rude. Never make fun of others.

Humbly follow God. He's the leader, so don't act like you are. He knows more than you, so don't act like He doesn't.

I will follow You, God. You make the path, give directions, and always walk with me. Help me to be fair, kind, and humble.

HOME TEACHING

Hear your father's teaching, my son, and do not turn away from your mother's teaching.
PROVERBS 1:8

★

God has put adults in your life who can teach you things. Today's verse talks about dads and moms; but you might have a grandparent, an aunt or uncle, or maybe a foster parent who helps you. Don't ignore them. Don't make fun of them.

Adults aren't perfect. Neither are you. Only God is perfect. The adults He put in your life—who care about you the most—will always help you. And God wants you to pay attention. Believe it or not, some people treat the adults in their life with disrespect. God says not to do that.

Part of being kind and walking humbly with God is doing what He asks. Listen and don't run the other way. Learn from Him—because it's worth it!

Make the right choice. Do what God asks you to do today—at home or wherever you are!

I want to obey the adults You've put in my life to help me, Father. Teach me and lead me. I want to follow where You're going.

QUEST INSTRUCTIONS

Do not act like the sinful people of the world. Let God change your life. First of all, let Him give you a new mind. Then you will know what God wants you to do. And the things you do will be good and pleasing and perfect.
ROMANS 12:2

This book is filled with instructions for your quest to follow God. Each devotion invites you to move forward in your walk with Him. After all, it doesn't make sense to say, "Follow God," but then not show you *how* to do it. The encouragement to "follow God" is great advice, but it could leave you confused if it's not explained.

By reading the Bible, you can learn what God wants. Take today's verse, for example: "Do not act like the sinful people of the world." There are already enough sinful people, so try something different: "Let God change your life." How? "Let Him give you a new mind." How can that help? "You will know what God wants you to do." And who doesn't want to know that?

I can make progress in the life I want to live for You, God. When I know what You want, I can make the right choice to follow You. Please teach me.

SEEK WISDOM

Teach young men to be wise.
Titus 2:6

★

Wisdom isn't like a certificate you get for listening to someone who's super smart. It's not a degree you earn by reading lots of thick books. It's not even simply learning good lessons from your mistakes. If you want to be wise, you use your mind to consider information. You use your heart to connect with the information you learn. And you use your spirit to understand what to do with that information. We can gain a boatload of wisdom from the words in the Bible.

Wisdom is a mixture of learning and understanding and then doing something with what you learn and understand. Don't stop with just discovering facts. Don't stop with saying, "Well, that makes sense." Do something more! Let God's truth change the way you do things.

God wants you, as a young man, to be taught wisdom. His goal is for you to become wise.

You haven't left me to try to figure things out on my own, Lord. You have wisdom and want to share it with me. I can know what You want. I can decide to obey. I can. I should. I will!

BE LIKE THAT

Be like those who have faith and have not given up.
HEBREWS 6:12

★

To have faith means that you believe that what *will* happen is better than what you think. Faith trusts when it would be easier to worry. Faith lets God have control over things that seem out of control.

Be full of faith! Be a believer—a truster. Be a boy who's willing to let God take charge. Be someone who really believes God can be trusted with any problem.

Never give up. Don't stop trying, because God is *never* done teaching. There's always a new lesson to learn, a new nugget of wisdom to consider, and a new insight awesome enough to inspire a "Thank You, God!"

You could be like foolish people, who don't believe in God. They always give up. But being foolish will get you nowhere. Believing God gives you courage and strength.

I want to be like people who believe in You, Father. Giving up means I don't think You can or will help me. You have promised to help. And I know You can be trusted.

DO WHAT IS GOOD AND RIGHT

Be strong. Do not allow anyone to change your mind. Always do your work well for the Lord. You know that whatever you do for Him will not be wasted.
1 CORINTHIANS 15:58

★

It's easy to believe that what other people think about you is very important. Sometimes God will ask you to do something that's good and right, but it's not something other people think you should do. That's when you need to remember that God should *always* be the One you're most interested in pleasing.

When you're following God, don't let those who disagree with you change your mind. Your efforts, talents, and strength are *never* wasted when you use them for God.

Do your best to learn what God wants you to do; then do what He wants, as if He's the only One watching. He's pleased when you trust Him enough to obey.

I don't want to try to make everyone happy, Lord. I only want to please You! Help me follow You, so I can be in the right place to do the right thing at the right time.

A WORRIED HEART

Do not worry. Learn to pray about everything. Give thanks to God as you ask Him for what you need. The peace of God is much greater than the human mind can understand. This peace will keep your hearts and minds through Christ Jesus.

PHILIPPIANS 4:6–7

Instructions are written to explain and show you how to do things the right way. If you don't follow them, you could put something together the wrong way. The finished product might not look like it's supposed to, or you might have leftover parts. You might feel anxious and frustrated if something you need to put together doesn't come with instructions.

God gave us a book called the Bible. It's filled with instructions, and it promises customer support if you get stuck. God will help you when you don't understand.

In today's verse, the instruction is to stop worrying. You can do that by praying about everything—even about those things that don't make you worry.

Thank You, Father, for Your instructions in the Bible. I can always ask You for the things I need. Thanks for the peace You send when I pray. My heart wants to worry, but praying helps with that. Thank You for taking away my worried heart.

HAPPY TO SEE YOU TRIP

Keep awake! Watch at all times. The devil is working against you. He is walking around like a hungry lion with his mouth open. He is looking for someone to eat.
1 PETER 5:8

★

The devil doesn't want you to follow God. He does everything he possibly can to convince you to stay away from God. And sometimes he succeeds. *Don't let him.*

God is good—the devil isn't. God wants the best for you—the devil doesn't. God wants to rescue you—the devil wants to destroy you. Pay attention to things that could cause you to turn your back on God. Maybe you have friends who make fun of God or make fun of you, or maybe you've been tempted to take the side of someone who doesn't like God. This is what today's verse means when it says that the devil is "like a hungry lion with his mouth open." He's happy to see you trip in your quest, and he would be thrilled to see you stay down.

Ask God to help you stand up against the devil. And He will!

Help me pay attention, God. Help me keep looking for signs of danger. Please rescue me!

HEAR; THEN DO

Obey the Word of God. If you hear only and do not act, you are only fooling yourself.

JAMES 1:22

★

Your mom tells you to clean your room. She tells you that if you clean your room, you can do that fun thing you planned with your friend. But if you don't clean your room, that privilege goes away. You heard the very clear terms. Did you choose to obey? Maybe. Maybe not.

God gives you instructions. A better life is on the line. If you follow instructions, greater opportunities will be available to you. If you don't follow instructions, you'll have fewer opportunities and need more training. You heard God's clear terms. Have you obeyed? Maybe. Maybe not.

If all you do is listen and say, "Well, that's interesting," then you've decided to take in information without making a commitment. You're fooling yourself if you think God likes this response. Deciding to follow God's instructions is an act of obedience. Obedience leads to faithfulness. Faithfulness leads to greater opportunity.

Obeying my parents can help me see that I need to do more than just listen to information about You, Father. I want to follow Your instructions and make good decisions.

HE'S NEVER MADE A MISTAKE

Trust in the Lord with all your heart, and do not trust in your own understanding. Agree with Him in all your ways, and He will make your paths straight.
PROVERBS 3:5–6

Every choice you've ever made has been a good one, right? Well, maybe not *every* choice. But God? He's never made a bad choice. *Ever.* So if you have to choose between trusting yourself and trusting God, you should choose the One who's never made a mistake.

The things you think you know are nothing compared to what God knows. He knows everything that has happened, everything that is happening right now, and everything that will happen in the future. God is all-knowing and wise.

Trust Him. Agree that His instructions are good, and then watch Him move you to the place you need to be. It's a better place than where you are right now. That's a promise!

I don't make perfect decisions, Lord, so it doesn't make sense for me to trust myself to do something I've never been able to do. Help me trust You instead. Teach me and help me do the things You instruct me to do.

RECOGNIZE HIS LOVE

Love each other with a kind heart and with a mind that has no pride.
1 PETER 3:8

★

God doesn't try to prove He's God. He *knows* He's God. He wants you to make the choice to believe it's true. He asks you to believe He can rescue you and then waits for you to say, "I need to be rescued." He loves you and waits for you to recognize His love. He's kind and will wait for you to recognize His kindness. Acknowledging God's goodness will lead you to turn away from trusting yourself and turn you toward trusting Him—the God who is humble, loving, and kind.

You're unique—different from everyone else. God made you that way. But to become a friend, you'll need to learn how to put others before yourself. You can be humble. You can love others. You can be kind.

You never want me to be confused, Father. You knew I would need to be kind, so You told me to be kind. I need to love others, so You told me to love. I need to be humble, so You told me not to brag. Help me learn to put others first.

THE WORDS AREN'T GENUINE

"When you pray, do not be as those who pretend to be someone they are not. They love to stand and pray in the places of worship or in the streets so people can see them."
MATTHEW 6:5

★

Prayer is talking to God about the things that bother you, the good things He has done, and the people who need His help. Prayer isn't about impressing people. You can make prayer that way (and you wouldn't be the first to do so), but God says to stay away from using a God conversation to get a human compliment.

God says praying to impress others is pretending—it's an act, and it isn't genuine.

You pray to a God who loves to hear what's on your heart; but if you're praying to impress other people, then maybe you're not really talking to God. He's listening, but the feelings in your heart and the thoughts on your mind are never actually shared. This kind of prayer isn't effective, and it makes God sad.

Pray real prayers. Share what's on your heart with God right now.

I want my prayers to be real, Lord. Help me remember I'm talking to You and not joining a drama club.

PEOPLE HURT PEOPLE

[Jesus said,] "I say to you, My friends, do not be afraid of those who kill the body and then can do no more."

LUKE 12:4

★

Sometimes people hurt people. You might know what that's like. It could be a bully at school, a brother or other family member, or even a stranger. People make bad choices—God calls these bad choices *sin*.

But God has some interesting instructions for those moments when someone hurts you. Don't be afraid—there's no need. No one can stop God's love for you. They can't threaten God to make Him stop forgiving you. They can't even change His plans.

Sure, people can be annoying and can make you feel angry or sad. They can cause pain. They may never seem to feel sorry. But no matter how hard they try, they can never change the way God feels about you. So stop being afraid. Trust God to arrive in time to comfort you and give you the strength to keep on this amazing adventure that leads to Him.

I don't want to be hurt, Father;
but when I am, help me remember that
any pain I feel will be outweighed by all
the wonderful gifts You have for me.

HUNGER, THIRST, AND WORRY

[Jesus said,] "Do not give so much thought to what you will eat or drink. Do not be worried about it."
LUKE 12:29

Juice or soda? Chicken or hamburger? Fruit or veggies? There are so many decisions about food and drink. Some foods and beverages you love; others you're not so crazy about. Sure, you need food and drink, but God said neither are worth worrying about. Even when food is scarce, worrying about it won't change what you ultimately get to eat.

It's okay to have your favorite foods, but don't complain when you're served something else to eat. You probably won't remember a week from now what you ate for tonight's dinner. You can enjoy food when you eat it and forget it by your next meal! God says there's no value in worrying about food or drink.

Gratitude is much better than complaints. God knows what you need, and what you need may not always be your favorite meal.

It's disappointing when I can't get what I want, Lord. There are so many kinds of food at the store and at the drive-through. Help me to be grateful for what You provide and to worry less about what's on the menu.

WISE BY LEARNING

Live in peace with each other. Do not act or think with pride. Be happy to be with poor people. Keep yourself from thinking you are so wise.

ROMANS 12:16

★

Being around people who are a lot like you can make you feel comfortable and accepted. But God has given instructions about living with and around all kinds of people.

"Live in peace with each other." Don't let even a *silent* war keep you at odds with anyone.

"Do not act or think with pride." If you do, you may begin to believe you're more important than other people. God says that kind of thinking is a lie.

"Be happy to be with poor people." God could have said to be happy to be with rich people. But He didn't. There shouldn't be just one type of person you want to be around.

"Keep yourself from thinking you are so wise." Become wise by learning from God. Don't ever let yourself believe that you're the smartest person in the room.

When I feel like comparing myself to someone else, remind me I should compare myself to You, Father. Then I will remember that I don't know even a fraction of what You know.

GROW UP, BUT DON'T "GROW UP"

Do not be like children in your thinking. Be full-grown, but be like children in not knowing how to sin.

1 CORINTHIANS 14:20

★

God wants you to grow up—*and* be a kid. He's not confused, although you might be.

As you follow God's instructions, you'll grow up in the thoughts you think and the decisions you make. God wants that for you.

Why would God want you to make decisions that don't line up with His instructions? Why would He say, "*Follow Me*," but never give you instructions on how to do that?

God gives you *everything* you need to grow up as a Christian. He doesn't leave anything out. The only thing that can stop you from growing up is you. You can refuse to learn. You can refuse to follow God's instructions.

God doesn't want you to stay immature, but He does want you to stay innocent by obeying His instructions. Grow up, but don't "grow up."

I want to grow up, Lord God. I want my choices to be the choices You want for me. I don't want to experience sin just so I know what sin is like.

THE CLEAR QUEST

Do not be foolish. Understand what the Lord wants you to do.
Ephesians 5:17

God has given instructions for so many things. Guessing what He wants is a waste of time. Ignoring His instructions leads to breaking His rules. That's a foolish choice.

God has things for you to do. Be involved in the things He's doing. You can begin to understand His plans for you specifically when you learn what He wants for all His followers. Wisdom comes when you act on what you know about His plans. The instructions you read here are a small sample of the instructions God has for you. To really know what God wants, you'll need to read the Bible.

If you wear glasses to help you see better, then it becomes much harder to take a test if you don't have your glasses. You need to see clearly to read clearly. You also need to see clearly to know God's path for you in this ongoing quest. See, read, and think—clearly.

I think I'm beginning to understand how I can make better choices when I know what You want, Father. Help me learn, understand, and act on Your instructions in a way that tells You and others that I'm following You.

DON'T GET TIRED

Do not get tired of doing good.
2 THESSALONIANS 3:13

Doing good is God's idea. He has been doing good forever. He has never stopped. But God also knew that while *He* wants you to do good, *you* might not always want to. That's why He gave instructions.

Do good. Keep doing good. Don't get tired of doing good.

Sound hard? It is! It's much easier to be selfish. You'll want to take a break from doing good. That doesn't necessarily mean you'll want to do bad things. You may just get tired of being helpful. God doesn't want you to make a bad choice simply because you don't feel like doing something.

If an adult asks you to make your bed, it's never a good idea to say, "I don't feel like it." You may not feel like doing it, but you've been given instructions to follow—and you're expected to follow them, even if you'd rather be doing something else.

Good things happen when you make the choice to do good.

Help me do good because it's the right thing to do, Lord God. I want to be helpful because You have helped me.

WHEN YOUR BRAIN HASN'T THOUGHT

Jesus said to them all, "Watch yourselves! Keep from wanting all kinds of things you should not have. A man's life is not made up of things, even if he has many riches."

LUKE 12:15

★

Maybe you've heard someone say, "Think before you speak." Some people wonder if your mouth can say things your brain hasn't even thought of yet. That can seem like a good possibility, because the things you say *can* get you into trouble—and they have, right?

God wants you to pay attention to what you're doing and to be careful about the choices you make. After you've paid attention, think about whether what you're doing brings you closer to God or moves you in a different direction.

Sometimes you might start acting like it's Christmas, wanting to have everything you see. Yet the things you want may not be the things you need. What you need are things only God can give—and His gifts last forever.

Carefully chosen words are the words I want to speak, Father. Help me remember that Your gifts are so much better than anything on my wish list.

I GOTTA SHARE THIS

There is one who is free in giving, and yet he grows richer. And there is one who keeps what he should give, but he ends up needing more.
PROVERBS 11:24

★

When God is the One giving, then you'll always have more than you need. When He gives you His love, He gives more than you need—so share it! When He gives you His forgiveness, it can open your heart to do for others exactly what God has done for you—*forgive*.

When you readily give what others need, you're telling God, "Give me more. I gotta share this!"

On the other hand, maybe you don't really believe you're fully loved by God. You don't recognize God's gift, so you can't share it. When God offers to forgive you, but you think you've made too many bad choices, you'll struggle to forgive others because you've never experienced true forgiveness yourself.

With God, you're rich to begin with, so giving from the extra should be easy. It's what God calls *freedom*.

Lord, I want to feel the freedom that comes when I'm not greedy. You've given me so much. I don't want to keep anything that You want me to share.

WHO SHOULD CHANGE YOUR MIND

Be careful that no one changes your mind and faith by much learning and big sounding ideas. Those things are what men dream up. They are always trying to make new religions. These leave out Christ.

COLOSSIANS 2:8

★

Have you ever said that you believe something is true only to have someone else say, "I don't think so"? You didn't expect that. They explain why they think you're wrong, and you might choose to stop believing what you thought was true and start believing the new thing you just heard. But what if you stopped believing something God said is true? Then you've chosen to believe a lie!

God's instructions say that letting other people change your mind about Him is easy to do, but it's wrong. Anyone who leaves God out of what they believe should not be someone you follow. You should never accept their arguments.

Stand strong for God, who gives truth, teaches truth, and *is* absolute truth.

If You don't say something is true, then I should be careful about believing it, Father. Help me read Your Word to know Your truth.

I'M SORRY

"Be sorry for your sins, turn from them,
and believe the Good News."
MARK 1:15

★

If you've ever hurt someone's feelings, you've probably heard an adult tell you that you need to say, "I'm sorry." Bad behavior needs to be followed with an apology—and you should mean what you say. But saying, "I'm sorry," doesn't always mean you feel like you've done something wrong. It might just be something you say so you can move on.

God wants you to be sorry for breaking His rules. He doesn't ask you to just say, "I'm sorry." God wants you to *be* sorry. God is never interested in hearing you say words you don't really mean.

You might believe that it's okay to offer God your list of bad choices today—and then start a new list of bad choices to tell Him about the next time you pray. God loves to see genuine sorrow when you recognize you've broken His rules. He's happy when your apology means you really do intend to walk away from the same bad choices.

Please stay close to me, Lord. Help me to make new and better decisions that show I want to follow You. I want You to lead me.

PART-TIME WORRIER

"Look at the birds. They do not plant seeds. They do not gather grain. They have no grain buildings for keeping grain. Yet God feeds them. Are you not worth more than the birds?"

LUKE 12:24

★

A robin doesn't push a cart into the grocery store and review the labels on a box of granola bars. A sparrow doesn't make a list of what it needs for the next week. An eagle doesn't do any online shopping for food. Why? They don't need to—God feeds them.

How often do you pay attention to birds? They fly just outside your window, usually with no one watching. They don't store food like squirrels. They don't gather a bunch of food and rent storage lockers to keep it safe. They have enough food and don't seem to worry about where their next meal will come from.

The problem is you're probably at least a part-time worrier. You might worry about food, clothes, or what the weather is going to do tomorrow. You might worry about your health, the bully at school, or being alone in the dark. Worry is easy. But don't worry. . .be a bird instead!

You said I'm worth more than birds, Father. You take care of them, so I know You can (and will) take care of me. Thank You!

NO MORE SHRINK AND SHRIVEL

[God said to Joshua,] "Be strong and have strength of heart! Do not be afraid or lose faith. For the Lord your God is with you anywhere you go."
JOSHUA 1:9

★

When you worry, something shrinks inside. Where you're afraid, your courage somehow shrivels. God has a way to fix that. The first thing you should know is that God doesn't ask you to schedule your conversation with Him to make sure He's available to listen. There may be a time of day when it seems more natural to pray; but God is available anytime, any day, for any reason.

If faith is a tire, don't let it lose air. If it's a coat, keep it in good shape. And if it's a race, then never ever stop running. Faith is a belief in God that tells fear it's not welcome.

Because God started this quest, He'll stay with you every step of the way. Walk with Him—not away from Him. Be courageous. Be strong.

I want to look for You, Lord. I want to listen for You, follow You, and learn more about where You're leading me. Make me strong. Help me to obey.

KEEP WATCHING, STOP WORRYING

You must keep praying.
Keep watching! Be thankful always.
COLOSSIANS 4:2

★

Yesterday you read that God tells you not to worry, but today His instructions tell you to keep watching. You might make the mistake of thinking God is confused. *He's not.*

Yes, you should pay attention to the things happening around you. When you do, you notice more things to pray for, and you can help when help is needed—because you were paying attention. Keeping watch also might mean that you're ready to step up. Watching is an action.

On the other hand, worry just rolls like a snowball in your mind. You can't take action because you're scared. You can only think about how bad your situation could get—with no plan for how to get through it. Worry makes you feel helpless.

Watching offers opportunity. Worry makes you hide alone. Watching believes God has a plan. Worry wonders if God can help.

God's instructions? Keep watching. Stop worrying.

I can worry about everything, Father, but it keeps me from watching. Or I could watch, and then maybe I wouldn't worry so much. Help me trust You more.

EVERYONE

Love each other as Christian brothers.
Show respect for each other.
ROMANS 12:10

★

Today's verse seems simple, doesn't it? Love and respect other people. But many people struggle to follow these instructions. "Love people who are mean?" Yes. "Respect people who are rude?" Yes. "Love and respect people I'm not even sure I like?" Yes. See, these are simple instructions that you might have trouble following.

You might want to obey. You might believe you can. You might even think it's a great idea. But then you're face-to-face with someone who, for whatever reason, seems hard to love. Does God really mean you should love *them*? Yes!

Today's verse mentions loving other Christians, but God didn't limit these instructions to only those who love Jesus. Mark 12:30–31 even says you should love God and then love everyone else. That's the instruction—*everyone*. No one is left out.

Because God loves all people, He expects you to do the same.

I'm not You, Lord. I don't know how I can love everyone; but because You love me, I want to learn how. Please teach me so I can follow Your instructions.

NO LONGER IMPOSSIBLE

*[Jesus said,] "I tell you, love those who hate you. (*Respect and give thanks for those who say bad things to you. Do good to those who hate you.) Pray for those who do bad things to you and who make it hard for you."*

MATTHEW 5:44

★

People will say bad things about you; others will hate you. God's instructions yesterday were to love and respect others. The instructions continue today—do good things for others and pray for them.

Today's instructions seem impossible, don't they? If God doesn't help you, then you can't love those who hate you. Fairness is something you're learning, so you believe that you share with people who share with you. You love people who love you. You respect people who respect you. Then? . . . You pray for those who share with, love, and respect you too. God says that's not enough—you need to include *everyone*! But you can't do it on your own. What God asks might not seem fair, but remember God loved you when you refused to love Him.

You're my example, Father. When it seems impossible to love, You prove that You can take the impossible and make it possible.

MORE THAN KIND AND NICE

"Do for other people what you would like to have them do for you."
LUKE 6:31

God must really want you to care about other people. Love, respect, do good, and pray for people. Today God brings this instruction to an even deeper place.

It may not be enough to just be kind and nice to other people. God wants you to think about the things that would make you happy if someone did those same things for you. Once you have those things in your mind, God wants you to treat other people the way you want to be treated. You want good things for yourself, so you should do good things for other people. You want to be respected, so you should respect others. You want to be loved, so you should love others. You want people to pray for you, so you should pray for others. Do these things for people before they do anything for you. In fact, go ahead and do these things *even if* they never do anything for you. God will notice.

You have done what You're asking me to do, Lord. You want me to follow Your example because others need to see You in me.

ONE OF THE MAIN THINGS

Nothing should be done because of pride or thinking about yourself. Think of other people as more important than yourself.
PHILIPPIANS 2:3

When you stop thinking about other people and only think about what you want, you can get confused about what God wants you to do. You could refuse to love others because you're thinking about what you want; or you could make it look like you love, respect, do good, and pray just so people will notice. But neither of those things is the right thing to do.

God made you one of a kind. He loves you. He sent Jesus to pay the price for your sin. He thinks a lot about you—so you don't have to. See other people as important and worth caring about too. Make caring for other people a priority in your life.

God takes care of you and asks you to help take care of others. That's hard to do when you don't take time to think of ways you can help. Follow His lead today and every day!

Teach me how to care for people, Father. Help me pay attention to Your instructions. Please use my hands and feet to help others.

THE THINGS YOU DO

Let us not love with words or in talk only.
Let us love by what we do and in truth.
1 JOHN 3:18

Maybe you've heard someone say that love is a verb. That means love is more than words or feelings. A verb is any word that describes action. Love does something. If you make the choice to love, you back it up with action.

What does that look like? Well, if you love your mom, you might put your love into action by making your bed, taking out the trash, or feeding your pets. Love is never just the words you say; it's also the things you do. Love doesn't just show up when you feel like it—love either shows up or hides with every choice you make. How you feel about someone has nothing to do with love. Your choices will show the truth. Either you love (through what you do) or you don't. God says love is a choice that does something for others.

Saying "I love you" isn't always the same as truly loving people. God, give me the courage to really love others in what I say and do.

DOES IT HONOR GOD?

Whatever you do. . .honor God.
1 CORINTHIANS 10:31

★

You can make good decisions by asking yourself one question: "Is what I'm about to do something that would honor and please God?" If the answer is no, then don't do it. But this is one of those easy ideas that's actually hard to do.

If you wonder if it makes sense to cheat, ask yourself, "Would cheating honor or please God?" If the answer is no, then don't cheat. The hard part is when you're stuck on a question and you think cheating is the only way you can get it right. You already know you can—and should—study before a test, but you can also pray and ask God to help you remember what you studied. That honors and pleases God. Cheating does not.

Ask the question when you wonder if it's okay to leave people out, pick on someone, or take something that doesn't belong to you. If it doesn't honor God, don't do it!

I haven't always thought to ask if the things I do please You, Father. Give me the wisdom to stop and ask before doing something I'll later wish I could take back.

LOVE ENOUGH TO SHARE

"Give, and it will be given to you. You will have more than enough. . . . The way you give to others is the way you will receive in return."
LUKE 6:38

★

Generosity means a willingness to give. When you're generous, expect God to be generous with you. You give, and God gives something back. To understand how that works, think about going to the store. Maybe you want some baseball cards. You get the cards, go to the checkout, and give the cashier some money. What you get in return isn't money but cards.

When you give to others, you probably aren't going to get exactly what you gave. If you give time, you might get back the good feeling that comes with helping someone. If you give money, you might get back the blessing of a new friend.

Give and you'll get—but not always what you give and not always at the same time you give. It is *always* worth the choice to love enough to share with others.

Lord, please help me to follow Your instructions without worrying about what I might get for helping. I want to be generous. I want to be grateful.

THE "NOT SO GREAT" AND THE "VERY BAD"

Always give thanks for all things to God the Father in the name of our Lord Jesus Christ.
EPHESIANS 5:20

★

No one gets to tell God, "I don't have to follow Your instructions." Someday you'll be a man, and you might even have children who will need to see their daddy doing the right thing. This is especially true for those who want their children to follow God. You can be an example for your children and other young people in your life to follow. They will look to you to show them the right thing to do.

Today's instruction is to give thanks to God and leave nothing out. It's easy to thank God for the good things that happen. Those things are easy to remember—because good things are meant to be shared. But you should also thank Him for the not-so-great things and the very bad things. Why? Because God often uses those things to teach you what He wants you to know, and He also works to bring good from those not-so-great or bad things. So always start your prayer by saying "Thank You."

Thank You, Father. I have been given good things and I have lived through bad things, but You are always with me—and that's a very good thing.

SERIOUS ABOUT OBEYING

Work at it so everyone may see you
are growing as a Christian.
1 TIMOTHY 4:15

★

Doing good things to impress people is a bad idea. You know that because you've read it in God's Word, but that doesn't mean you stop doing good things. And it could be true that people will notice, but not because you're trying to show off. God wants people to notice that you are growing up as a Christian. Then they will learn to trust you. They might even thank God that you're becoming serious about obeying His instructions.

Christians need to grow because God uses grown-up Christians to lead. He wants them to be examples to those who are still growing. You aren't expected to be grown up yet, but God wants others to "see you are growing as a Christian."

Are you trying to get people to notice you, or are you doing your best to make God famous? Do you want people's eyes on you—or on God?

Lord God, please help me to follow You. Help me to learn from Your wisdom. Help me to be brave in Your strength. Be my teacher today, tomorrow, and forever.

GIVE THAT WAY

"You have received much, now give much."
MATTHEW 10:8

★

God gave to you before you ever considered giving to anyone else. He gave you life, people to care for you, and a place to stay. *He was just getting started.* He gave you love when you didn't know how to love. He gave you forgiveness when you struggled to forgive someone who hurt you. He gave you a future when all you could think about was today. He gave, gave some more, and then kept on giving.

Now you're in a place where you've been given more than you might expect. You breathe air and have food to eat and water to drink. God is the One who made them. It's easy to think these good things will always just be there. But they wouldn't be if it weren't for God.

Pay attention to what He's doing and then follow His example. He gives—so you give. He doesn't stop giving—so keep giving. He gives even when you don't do anything to deserve it—so give that same way.

Giving is Your idea, Father. Help me do what You've always done. Help me show Your love by giving the things I've received from You.

PLENTY TO GIVE AWAY

God can give you all you need. He will give you more than enough. You will have everything you need for yourselves. And you will have enough left over to give when there is a need.

2 CORINTHIANS 9:8

There is more air than you can breathe, more food than you can eat, and more water than you can drink. Trying to keep it all for yourself is unwise. God has given you more than you can use so that you have plenty to give away. What you really need, God has taken care of.

It's easy to get caught up in the fact that God is good (He is), that He provides (He does), and that there is more than enough (there always has been). Once the importance of those thoughts sinks in, God wants His family to stay on the lookout for the needs around them. And then? . . . Give!

You want me to share, Lord. In today's verse, I'm given all the reasons I need to be generous. I want to remember that the verse instructs me to "give when there is a need."

MORE TO GIVE AWAY

It is God Who gives seed to the man to plant. He also gives the bread to eat. Then we know He will give you more seed to plant and make it grow so you will have more to give away.

2 CORINTHIANS 9:10

★

Farmers plant seeds and look after the crops. They get rid of weeds, make sure the plants are watered, and eventually harvest the crop. They usually get much more than they planted. Farmers do a lot to make sure everyone is fed. But God created the seed, makes it grow, and provides more than the farmer planted. He makes the sun to shine, sends rain, and gives the farmer the wisdom to farm.

You might think this means that God wants you to work hard so you can have more things, more time, or more money. Don't miss the end of today's verse. God gives so that "you will have more to give away."

You have a special plan for the things You provide, Father. The more You give, the more I can share. The things I'm blessed with can bless others. The extra may be just what You can use to help others.

MANY WILL GIVE THANKS

God will give you enough so you can always give to others. Then many will give thanks to God for sending gifts through us.

2 CORINTHIANS 9:11

★

This story about giving has been growing over several days. Giving is God's gift, but it's also what He wants from you. He gives extra so you won't miss out if you share what He gives. In this close look at giving, you've discovered the reason God wants you to give. The answer is in the last sentence of today's verse: "Many will give thanks to God for sending gifts through us."

Giving is a choice you make because of an instruction from God to be generous. You keep the attention on God, who started the gift giving. You treat people with respect as you honor God. People just might notice that what you've done was God's way of answering their prayer and "will give thanks to God." You can be happy knowing your gift has honored God.

I know You work through people who understand what giving can do, Lord. Help me understand and grow in generosity.

AVOID REPLACEMENTS

[God said,] "Have no gods other than Me."
EXODUS 20:3

★

Everyone gets distracted. They have something they need to do, but something stops them. Their steps go a different way, and they forget what they were doing. Important things become less important. It might seem like it would be okay to take a break from God, but *it's not.*

When you take a break from God, you're saying that something else is more important than He is. If something is more important than God, then it has taken His place. This means the God who made you—the One who takes care of you and knows where you could be if you had continued to follow Him—must wait for you to remember Him. Why be rude? Don't let *anything* come between you and God. Pay attention and make good decisions; and when you fail, tell God about it and ask for His help.

No matter how interesting new things are, they'll never be a replacement for God. *Never.*

I don't want a wall to stand between You and me, Father. May I move in the direction Your steps lead and know You as the only God worth following.

THE RIGHT THING

"You must love the Lord your God with all your heart. You must love Him with all your soul. You must love Him with all your strength. You must love Him with all your mind."

LUKE 10:27

★

Do you remember reading that love is a verb? Love requires action. What you *do*—not how you *feel*—shows the true measure of your love.

Jesus didn't speak the words in today's verse, although they do sound like something He would have said. The words were spoken by an unnamed man who knew God's law. Jesus told him, "You have said the right thing. Do this and you will have life" (verse 28).

This man knew that loving God required heart, soul, strength, and mind. Each needed to be active in loving God. Each plays a role in the way you live your life and make decisions.

Loving God isn't just saying certain words. It's following, sharing, and helping. Loving God is learning His instructions and doing something about them.

You want all of me, Lord. Help me love You enough to give You every part of me. I want to be willing to do what You ask.

NO DOUBT

Jesus said to them, "Have faith in God."
MARK 11:22

There was never a question in the minds of people who spent time with Jesus—He wanted them to trust His Father. He didn't want them to doubt. He wanted them to discover His peace.

Jesus trusted God, and people noticed. He followed God, and people were inspired to walk with Him. He didn't doubt, and that's where people struggled.

You might doubt God for all kinds of reasons. You might think He's too good to be true. You might worry what will happen if you *do* trust Him. You might be tempted to listen to other people who think believing in Him is a bad idea.

Believing is a choice only you can make for yourself. God doesn't want you to doubt. He doesn't want you to worry. He doesn't want you to think that following Him is only a good idea if your friends agree.

Have faith in God. Let Him take your worry and doubt and replace them with peace and confidence in His goodness.

If it's hard for me to trust You, Father, it must be hard for others. When I struggle, help me remember I'm not alone. I can trust You.

KINDNESS FOR PEOPLE WHO DON'T FOLLOW

Have loving-kindness for those who doubt.
JUDE 22

★

Jesus spent time with people who sinned. Then again, everyone sins (see Romans 3:23). Some thought they were better than most—and they thought Jesus should only spend time with people like them.

Christians should show loving-kindness to people who don't follow God yet. That can be hard when you want them to follow God *right now*.

Keep encouraging them to follow God, but never follow *their* example. If that sounds mean, you should look to the life of Jesus. He told people who sinned to stop sinning.

It's normal for people to doubt that God exists. Be patient. Giving up on people who doubt won't help them want to know more about God. They might just think that Christians don't like people who disagree with them. God said it was His kindness that drew people to Him (see Romans 2:4), so why would He want His family to be anything less than kind to others—even when they disagree?

I want to follow You and be kind to others, Lord. That's what You want for me too. May I serve You with my whole heart.

DOUBT MAKES THINGS HARD

Keep a strong hold on your faith in Christ.
1 TIMOTHY 1:19

★

If someone wants you to let go of faith, they introduce you to doubt. If you believe that God isn't really good—that He doesn't really love you and that He may not be worth following—then you spend time with doubt. The more time you spend with doubt, the easier it is to think God isn't very special.

Doubt always makes it hard to make good decisions. You'll second-guess almost everything. You'll think good choices will make life hard for you. You might even think there's no good thing in life. Who wants to live that way?

Take the leap to discover real faith. Hold on to it with everything you've got. Don't let doubt convince you to let go. Faith gives you a front-row seat to see all the ways God is faithful, loving, and kind. He always has been.

I don't want to get to know doubt, Father. Help me keep away from doubt and stay close to the trust You want me to have in You. Help me believe in You so I can go where You send me.

PRIDE RESISTED

Watch yourself! The person who thinks he can stand against sin had better watch that he does not fall into sin.

1 CORINTHIANS 10:12

★

You might feel like you're in a good place in your friendship with God. He means something to you, and you're willing to learn and grow. Believe it or not, there's a danger even in this place. The danger is that you might believe that sin is something you *used* to do but not anymore.

When you think these thoughts, you become proud of the fact that you're doing so well. You begin to notice other people who aren't having so much success. You compare what you do with what they do, and you think you're a better Christian than they are. You may even look down on people who struggle.

Pride is a sin. So when you find yourself feeling proud of how well you follow God, you need to be forgiven for pride. Pay attention. Think clearly. Ask God to help you resist pride.

I should never compare myself to other people, Lord. I'll never follow You perfectly. Be patient with me, and keep me humble.

THINK HIS THOUGHTS

Think as Christ Jesus thought.
PHILIPPIANS 2:5

★

Welcome to more impossible instruction from God's Word. Jesus was perfect; you are not. Jesus came to rescue; you needed rescue. Jesus knows everything; you'll work on gaining knowledge for the rest of your life. So how can you think the way He thinks?

This verse was given as lifetime instruction, so it's not as impossible as you might think. Thinking like Jesus means spending enough time with Him that you learn what He already thinks on all kinds of subjects. It also means you'll need to pray. Ask God to help you understand issues in the same way He understands them. He can help you see things the way He sees them.

God won't ever ask you to do something that He won't help you do. This is another instruction that's impossible—but only when you try to do it by yourself. Hint: Don't try to do it by yourself!

I can know more about what You want me to do when I understand why You want me to do it, Father. Help me understand the difference between the way I think and the way You think.

CHANGED FOR GOOD

Let the teaching of Christ and His words keep on living in you. These make your lives rich and full of wisdom. Keep on teaching and helping each other.
COLOSSIANS 3:16

When you were born, you started to grow physically—most people do. In the same way, when you were rescued from sin after you learned about God and accepted His new life, you started to grow spiritually—most people do. When the words God recorded in the Bible begin to live in your mind and heart, you should grow even more—and others should see it.

This instruction from the book of Colossians comes with a couple of promises: You'll have a rewarding life. And wisdom will spill over into every area of your life. Who doesn't want that?

Let God's Word change you. Make choices based on the change. Then? . . . Share what you're learning so other people can be helped—so other people can be changed.

Look for all the good things that happen when you follow God's instructions. Follow, and look for the good.

Learning about You is a good thing, Lord. I want to grow, share, and help others, knowing that what You have to teach me is exactly what I need to know.

ARE THEY LISTENING?

Speak with them in such a way they will want to listen to you. Do not let your talk sound foolish. Know how to give the right answer to anyone.
COLOSSIANS 4:6

★

The words you speak say a lot about you and what you believe. Your words can wound other people or cause them to turn away, or your words can inspire people to listen.

Sometimes people talk about God like He's the leader of a private club that only the most important people get into. Sometimes people talk about Jesus as though He only loves certain people. Sometimes people feel like they're being judged because they don't know Jesus yet.

Because God loves everyone, the people you interact with should know it. *Tell them.* Jesus came to rescue anyone who's willing to be rescued. That's a great point! God doesn't make you guess what He wants—His instructions are clear, and they're found in the Bible. This changes things.

You might be the first person to introduce someone to Jesus. Are they listening?

You want people to know You, Father.
Give me the words to say when I tell them about You.

USE YOUR WORDS

Watch your talk! No bad words should be coming from your mouth. Say what is good. Your words should help others grow as Christians.

EPHESIANS 4:29

★

Words can hurt or help. They're dark or light. They rip or repair. *Speak carefully.*

You've probably reacted to something mean someone said about you. It probably sounded like you took their insult and traded it for one of your own. Maybe you don't like each other now. That happens when two people speak words that don't help, that are dark, that rip apart. God's instructions are simple—be careful, little mouth, what you say. Your choices should show that you follow God. Your speech should be different than it used to be. Use the words you're learning to help other Christians grow up too.

Think about your words before you open your mouth. If they honor God and will help to make Him famous, then speak them. If they will hurt others because you want them to hurt, then keep your mouth shut. It will be hard, but mean words never help.

I've said words I wish I hadn't, Lord.
Make me strong enough to say,
"I'm sorry." Then let me tell You all about it.

THE NEED

Put out of your life all these things: bad feelings about other people, anger, temper, loud talk, bad talk which hurts other people, and bad feelings which hurt other people.

EPHESIANS 4:31

★

If you're wondering what things you should get rid of as a Christian, today's verse lists some items that should be left on the curb. Start early—take these things out now:

Bad feelings about other people. They make it hard to be a good friend.

Anger. Giving in to anger results in poor choices.

Temper. It's hard to be kind when your emotions seem volcanic.

Loud talk. Calling attention to yourself can be pretty awkward.

Bad talk that hurts other people. Share compassion instead.

Bad feelings that hurt other people. Doing things to hurt others is off limits.

Study the list in today's verse. God's way is better, and it always comes with the help to make the changes you need so you can develop more kindness. . .and so you can help others the way they need help.

I want to get rid of everything on Your list, Father. Help me remember this list so I know what not to pick up when I'm with friends.

ANSWERING THE "WHO"

Live your lives as the Good News of Christ says you should. . . . [Work] together as one, preaching the Good News.
PHILIPPIANS 1:27

★

The words you say and the things you do lead to either a life that's well lived or one you wish would've been different. God has provided instructions, but maybe you weren't paying attention.

If you're willing to give something a try, then today's set of quest instructions will remind you who you work for, who you work with, and who needs to know what you know. Fill in the following blanks.

Who you work for: ______________.

Who you work with: ______________.

Who needs to know what you know: ______________.

Take instructions from this book, and then keep reading God's Word for more. Hopefully, you will see how the past few days of instruction are building blocks for the way you live your Christian life—giving directions for you to follow and helping you offer hope to people who have never known real hope.

There are so many things You want me to experience, Lord. Help me soak in all Your instructions and discover that they always lead to adventure.

TELLING A LIE ABOUT GOD

The truth of God cannot be changed. It says, "The Lord knows those who are His." And, "Everyone who says he is a Christian must turn away from sin!"

2 TIMOTHY 2:19

★

What if you told someone, "I love basketball," and then they told everyone that what you really meant was you love ice cream? You might love ice cream, but that's not what you said. They're telling a lie and trying to make other people believe that you were telling a lie.

People do that all the time with God. He gives instructions, but people will say that He means something different than what He really said. Today's verse reminds you that God's truth can't be changed. You shouldn't modify it, lie about it, or say God didn't mean what He said. If God cannot lie, then what He instructs must be true.

You can't pick and choose what to believe about God. He tells you what He wants and who He is. Get to know Him. Believe what He says.

You speak truth and ask me to believe it, Father. Help me refuse to think that You don't really mean what You say.

NO CONFUSION

If you do not have wisdom, ask God for it.
He is always ready to give it to you and will
never say you are wrong for asking.
JAMES 1:5

★

Are you having trouble making a decision? Does it seem like it's hard to know the truth? Do you find yourself thinking, *I'm so confused*?

Imagine an instruction from God that says "*I can help you with that.*" This is what today's instruction does. When you don't know what to do, God instructs you to pray to Him and be courageous enough to ask Him for help so you know what you should do next.

Be thankful that God's Word says He's ready to help. He won't say that you made a mistake by asking for His help.

God isn't interested in making life hard for you. He wants you to make good decisions, so He will show you how. He wants you to know the truth, so He has given you His words in the Bible. God isn't confused—and He doesn't want you to be confused either.

I'm here, and I'm asking for help, Lord.
Teach me what I need to know. Show me how to be wise.

STOP BELIEVING HE WON'T SHOW UP

You must have faith as you ask Him. You must not doubt. Anyone who doubts is like a wave which is pushed around by the sea.

JAMES 1:6

If you've ever been on the ocean or in the middle of a lake, you've seen waves. Waves move in all kinds of directions. They might move forward or back, side to side, or even fall in on themselves. The sea tosses waves around like you might a ball.

God's instructions are clear: Don't pray like you're tossing a ball or watching a wave. Believe God will answer your prayers. When you doubt, you'll worry about whether God heard you or if He will answer your prayers.

When you feel like your prayer is going nowhere, you might be tempted to blame God; but you also might wonder how much you trust God. Don't doubt God. Don't fear that He won't answer. Stop thinking He won't show up.

I'll pray and You'll answer, Father. When I doubt You will answer, adjust my thinking and keep me trusting in You and Your promises.

TESTS AND TEMPTATION

When you are tempted to do wrong,
do not say, "God is tempting me." God cannot
be tempted. He will never tempt anyone.
JAMES 1:13

★

Today's instruction is in the form of information—information you can learn from. If you've ever wondered, while working through daily struggles, if God is the one tempting you to do something wrong, you now know He isn't. He doesn't tempt, hasn't tempted, and never will tempt anyone. He wants you to do the right thing—and He helps you do it. He is never happy when people sin, so why would He do something to make Himself unhappy? *He wouldn't.*

If you've ever had to do something in phys ed class to prove how physically fit you are, that's called a test. It's like a math or English test—but for your body instead of your mind. God's tests are for your spirit, but they never encourage you to break His rules. His tests help you see how well you're doing and where you still need to grow.

Lord, You are God, and You don't play
games with me. You speak the truth and
ask me to follow. When I don't follow,
help me remember that it was my choice.
Then? Help me choose to follow You again.

ANGER ISSUES

My Christian brothers, you know everyone should listen much and speak little. He should be slow to become angry.
JAMES 1:19

Did you know that being angry isn't a sin? Jesus was angry when visiting the temple. He found people treating God's house like it was a market. They were buying and selling things instead of worshipping God. That made Jesus upset. His anger was not sin.

When you're upset, you might be upset about the wrong things. You might do things when you're angry that God said you shouldn't do. You might refuse to forgive people, and that's something God *wants* you to do. The best advice might be exactly what God instructs—listen more, speak less, and don't make anger your first response.

Sometimes speaking your mind opens the door to anger; and when anger stays too long, its friends drop by—like envy, jealousy, and gossip. Long-term anger can make a huge mess, and the damage can last a very long time.

Before I get angry, Father, help me listen carefully and not jump to conclusions. Help me think before I speak. Help me remain calm when anger tempts me to lash out.

WHAT A WISE BOY LOOKS LIKE

Who among you is wise and understands? Let that one show from a good life by the things he does that he is wise and gentle.

James 3:13

Don't think of wisdom as just words someone speaks that sound wise. There are a lot of quotes that people use that aren't very wise at all—even though they sound good. Today's instructions say that the best way to show you are wise is through the decisions you make every day. People notice when you say something that sounds wise but then do something unwise. They want to know if what you say is what you do. Do your actions match up to your words?

Are you learning God's instructions? Are you following the instructions you're learning? Are you beginning to understand why those instructions are important to God?

Wisdom looks a lot like knowing what God says and then doing it.

Every day I make mistakes, Lord. I may not want to, but sometimes I still end up breaking Your rules. You have all wisdom, and You give us Your instructions in the Bible. Help me understand what Your Word says so I can gain wisdom.

GOOD DAYS + BAD DAYS = PRAYER DAYS

Is anyone among you suffering?
He should pray. Is anyone happy?
He should sing songs of thanks to God.
JAMES 5:13

★

Did something happen recently that made you frustrated or sad? Did something happen recently that brightened your whole day?

The struggles you face are similar to the struggles every other person faces. God cares about every single struggle; that's why He wants to hear from you in prayer. Bring your problems—no matter how big or small—and God will listen and offer comfort. If you pay attention, He'll give you answers in the Bible. The best news is that even when you're not sure what to do next, God will still stay with you, listen to you, and help you every minute of every day.

In the same way, the things that make you happy should bring you close to God. All blessings come from Him. Praying to give thanks is exactly the right response to good days.

I have no excuse not to pray, Father. When I'm sad, I shouldn't hide from You. And when I'm happy, I shouldn't act like You had nothing to do with it.

WAIT A LITTLE LONGER

Learn well how to wait so you will be strong and complete and in need of nothing.
JAMES 1:4

Being patient is hard. You don't want to wait for something you *really* want. You don't want to wait for someone else to take you where you want to go. You don't want to wait to know things that you want to understand right now. But life isn't like a computer; you can't just click a button and have everything you want on demand. Learning is interactive. God gives instructions, and you probably have questions. He gives answers, and you might want to know more. That seems more like a friendship than a computer download, doesn't it? *A friendship is so much better!*

Learning to wait will help you develop patience. It will teach you compassion. It will even help you find value in the things God is teaching you.

God wants you to be patient. As you practice a willingness to wait, you will come to understand and trust that God has a very good future for you.

Help me wait for You, Lord. Help me trust that Your plan is worth the extra patience. Give me moments when I see the wisdom in my waiting.

WHAT LIPS TELL

Keep your tongue from sin and your lips from speaking lies.
PSALM 34:13

God offers two instructions in today's verse—although they might sound the same to you. The first is to keep your tongue from sin, and the second is to keep your lips from speaking lies. It's the difference between saying "Let's take something that's not ours" and "I didn't take anything that belonged to someone else." The first is a plan to deliberately break God's rules. The second is a lie to cover up your wrongdoing. God says both are wrong.

God has different goals for your words: He wants you to speak truth *and* make choices that honor Him. These instructions aren't just to make God happy. When you follow these instructions, others will see you as trustworthy and think you're worth believing. God will be honored when your lips tell the truth and your tongue shares His love.

It's easy to lie, Father. I've done it before, but You're never honored when I do. Keep me from thinking about sin, and keep my mouth from lying about my choices.

A FAIR TRADE

Rest in the Lord and be willing to wait for Him.
Do not trouble yourself when all goes well with
the one who carries out his sinful plans.

PSALM 37:7

★

What if God doesn't seem to say yes to your prayers when you want Him to? What if the thing He has planned is different from the thing you asked for? Are you okay with that?

On the other hand, what if you see someone who doesn't pray yet gets exactly what he wants? Do you think that's fair?

God's instructions in today's verse say that what God gives is better than anything you want. When someone gets exactly what they want, they never learn to wait for—or want—what God could give them.

Be content to wait for God's best, knowing He will satisfy your every need. When you don't wait for what you want right now, you just might get what you want and miss what you really need.

When I believe the best gifts come from You, Lord, then maybe I can be more willing to wait for the right time to receive Your good gifts.

SHOW AND TELL

O my people, hear my teaching. . . . Tell the children-to-come the praises of the Lord, and of His power and the great things He has done.

PSALM 78:1, 4

★

People who believe in Jesus and love Him aren't shy about celebrating who He is and what He has done. They tell others that God is good and that His greatness is awesome. He is strong and has accomplished countless wonderful things!

Celebrating the Lord is your job too. *Start today.* Tell others what you know about God. Start with your family and friends. Someday you can share about the Lord with your children and grandchildren too.

Learn to honor God and then—when the time comes—you can teach your children to do the same by showing them what praising God looks like. *Show your praise today.*

You're on a God-size adventure. It should last a lifetime, and the choices you make today can improve the lives of those around you now as well as the lives of all the members of your future family. *Don't wait to start.*

You're amazing, Father. Help me recognize it, celebrate it, and share it every day for the rest of my life. Others need to know. I don't want to keep You a secret.

REFUSING TO ANSWER

He who lives in the safe place of the Most High
will be in the shadow of the All-powerful.
PSALM 91:1

God is bigger than anything you're afraid of. His instructions are wiser than your guesses. His power is greater than your ambition. Live in God's *bigger*, *wiser*, and *greater* plan.

Don't be like someone who runs away from His safe place. Stay within His shadow. Being so close to Him means you have the best chance to hear when He speaks and follow where He leads.

How well are you protected when you keep running away from God? It's like having a phone but refusing to answer because it's God calling. He has instructions for you, but sometimes you won't listen. Sometimes you don't agree with God.

Today's verse is a challenge for you to stop running, start listening, and ultimately discover protection in the presence of God, who has more power than you can understand, more love than you'll ever need, and more direction than any map.

Let me talk with You and about You, Lord God. Let me listen when You're teaching, follow when You're leading, and rest when You're loving. Keep me close.

NO FEAR OF BAD NEWS

The man who is right and good will be remembered forever. He will not be afraid of bad news. His heart is strong because he trusts in the Lord.

PSALM 112:6–7

★

Who wants bad news? There's *bad* right in the name—bad news. Too often, bad news is linked with things you care about. Maybe you need to move, didn't make the team, or didn't get to hang out with friends. Maybe an adult in your life lost a job or had to go to the hospital. This is news no one wants to get—and that's why we call it *bad*.

But the good news is this: You don't need to be afraid of bad news. God's instructions sound easy, but you'll need God's help to have a strong heart. You need to be right with God and make good choices. When this describes you, you'll be able to trust that God can take your bad news and make it good.

You can turn around bad things to make them good, Father. Let me give all the bad things in my life to You. I want You to take care of the things I can't. Bring me good news, I pray.

WHAT HE SAYS

How can a young man keep his way pure? By living by Your Word.
PSALM 119:9

★

No boy goes to the store wanting a broken toy. Not many adults want a car that doesn't work. No one wants to live in a house with a hole in the roof.

Reading the Bible is what you do to get a clear picture of what God wants you to do and instructions on how God wants you to live. Purity is a characteristic of those who learn what God says and then do what He asks. They make the choice to live by following God's instructions that He has recorded in His Word, the Bible.

God didn't make you to be like a broken toy, car, or roof. You choose those things without His help. But when you invite God into the picture, you will find that broken things are repaired, old things become new, and dirty things get cleaned up. That's purity in action. That's what God does when you listen to what He says.

I can ask You to make me clean, Lord. But by reading Your Word, I'm saying I want to know You more. That's the best way for me to become pure.

PATH LIGHT

Your Word is a lamp to my feet and a light to my path.
PSALM 119:105

★

Today's verse is part of a prayer. It talks about the very things God was teaching the writer of this psalm. If you want to see where God wants you to go, you need to read what God says in His Word. If you can't see the path ahead and you're also trying to stay away from trouble, then knowing where you should take your next step is super important.

Maybe you wish you knew everything that will happen in your future; but there are a lot of steps between now and then, and often God only makes clear what step you need to take next. You don't get to know your entire story right now—because you're living it.

Without the light of God's Word and without God at his side, the writer of this psalm knew that any step he took would be in the wrong direction. He knew he needed God to guide him every step of the way.

I can imagine what my future will look like, Father, but You already know. Help me to follow the path You light up for me.

MEETING WITH GOD

Let us go with complete trust to the throne of God. We will receive His loving-kindness and have His loving-favor to help us whenever we need it.

HEBREWS 4:16

★

It's not just okay for you to come to God. He actually wants to spend time with you! It's like God says, "*There you are! I've been waiting for you.*"

You might be a little nervous. After all, you're talking to God. No one is bigger, better, stronger, wiser, holier, or more loving. *No one.* But God invites you to come to Him. You don't need an appointment, and you don't need to fill out any application forms to begin praying. God is so trustworthy that you can know for sure that He can't wait to spend time with you.

Don't be afraid. Don't hesitate. Don't make the decision to wait until you're older. Accept God's invitation and pray—right now. You need help, and God wants to help. Admit that you need what only God can give. Be bold. You have a meeting with God.

I don't know why You love me so much, Lord. I'm not perfect, and You are. Help me remember that You started this friendship. I'm overwhelmed. I'm grateful.

THE FAITH GIFT

Let us keep looking to Jesus. Our faith comes from Him.
HEBREWS 12:2

Maybe you're not surprised to read the instructions "Keep looking to Jesus." He is God's Son, after all. He came to rescue people just like you. You even learned yesterday that God wants rescued people to come to Him. So what are you waiting for?

Today's verse explains why you should pay so much attention to Jesus: "Faith comes from Him." Jesus asks you to have faith in Him, to trust Him, and to believe what He says. But it is Jesus who gives you the faith He asks for. You could ignore the faith He gives and put your trust in something else; but if you're wise, you'll reward His gift of faith by returning it to Him. The good news is that He doesn't stop giving faith, so you never have to stop believing. *Don't stop.*

Sometimes I think that if I give away trust too easily, Father, I will be hurt, because people tend to let other people down. But You are God, and Your Son gave me the gift of faith. Let me use that gift to trust You. I know You will never let me down.

THE WAY YOU TREAT GOD

Let us be thankful. Let us please God and worship Him.
HEBREWS 12:28

Think about an actor, singer, or professional sports player you really like. If you had the chance to spend a day with them, what would you say to them? Would you talk about the weather, struggles at school, or your last dental visit? Probably not. You'd want to know more about them. You'd want them to tell you more about what they do. That's what you're interested in knowing, right? You'd thank them for spending time with you and for making it a day worth remembering.

Be thankful that the God who made everything wants to spend time with you. When you spend time with Him, you get to know Him, ask questions, and tell Him how much you appreciate the amazing things He has done.

If you would do that for someone who is *not* God, why would you treat God as less special?

You do so much for me, Lord. I trust that You love me and want to spend time with me. It's the best news I've heard all day!

GOD'S TO-DO LIST

Let us love each other, because love comes from God. Those who love are God's children and they know God.
1 JOHN 4:7

★

On this important quest, you're learning more about God. You're learning what He wants you to do. If you're wise, you're asking for His help in getting His to-do list complete.

People can know you're growing up in your Christian faith when you're kind and compassionate and you show God's love to others. It's easy to point out the wrong things people do. . .to complain, criticize, and point to yourself as a better example of what a Christian looks like, but God doesn't ask you to do that. He asks you to do what He does—love people. Loving people is hard, so you'll need God's help; but when you love others genuinely, they will trust you more and want to know how you can love so freely. Love comes from God—it always has—and the people you meet need to know Him too!

I want to show Your love, Father. If it can change me, it can change anyone. They just need to see it first. Help me show it.

HE ALWAYS WILL BE

Do not love the world or anything in the world.
1 JOHN 2:15

★

God made the world, and He loves you. God made the ocean for you to enjoy but not to love. You can like video games, but you need to love God. He has always been most important. *He always will be.*

This planet you live on was created to get old. Metal rusts, clothing wears out, and buildings fall apart. You can shine things up, repair what's broken, and rebuild when needed; but that never completely stops something from no longer being useful—no matter how much you like it.

People aren't that way. And God isn't that way. God created you to be His friend. And He wants to be yours. When you love something that will fall apart more than you love God, you are neglecting a very important truth: You can love something that won't be around long, or you can love the God who has always been. *And always will be.* Only God can love you back.

Help me remember that real love is for people and You, Lord. This love is important. Everything else is just stuff to enjoy.

LIES

Stop lying to each other. Tell the truth.
EPHESIANS 4:25

When you love God and people, you don't want to lie to them. That doesn't show love. You could be afraid of getting in trouble, but God knows you've done something wrong before you ever tell Him—so don't wait. If you love your family, then tell them the truth even if it's uncomfortable. There will always be more trouble the longer you wait.

But there's more to the story. When you make a habit out of lying to people you're supposed to love—and when others notice you've been lying—you make it hard for others to trust you. But even more significant, you make it hard for others to believe that God is worth following. Why? Because people look at the way you act to decide if following God really makes a difference. If they can't see a difference in you, then maybe being a Christian doesn't matter. Of course, they'd be wrong, but that's the importance of your example. When you don't follow God's instructions, you should admit it and then make a change in your choices.

People know I make mistakes, Father.
Help me make choices that let people see
that I always come back to You.

THE LIFE YOU LEFT

Put away the old person you used to be.
Have nothing to do with your old sinful life.
EPHESIANS 4:22

★

It's possible you think you've always been pretty good. You haven't made terrible choices, you mostly obey, and you can't remember hurting others. It's true, some people have a lot of old life to put away, and it can take time. But be patient and remember that you have things to put away too.

Before you started following God, you tended to think about the things you wanted. Maybe you were selfish, told lies, and blamed other people for things they didn't do. Maybe you got away with it. Maybe it seemed normal.

God's instructions say that you are to "have nothing to do with your old sinful life." He didn't say, "*Try* not to have much to do with your old choices." He didn't say, "Just keep working on it." God said, "Have *nothing* to do with it."

That means you should never stop accepting God's help to make good decisions.

I don't want to settle for how things have always been, Lord. Help me become the new person You made me to be.

TIME FOR A DEEP CLEAN

Put out of your life these things also: anger, bad temper, bad feelings toward others, talk that hurts people, speaking against God, and dirty talk.
COLOSSIANS 3:8

Today's verse gives you a lot to think about. Getting rid of anger and other bad things can help you take steps away from your old life and make room for new thoughts and new actions.

Think of this like cleaning your room. You'll notice things you've held on to, but you're not sure why. You'll find stuff you should have thrown away collecting dust in a messy pile. Maybe there's something that stinks to everyone else, but you've left it because you like the fact that it annoys people.

Take a look at the room inside your heart. Are you stacking up anger, temper tantrums, bad feelings about others, hurtful words, negative thoughts about God, or jokes you know you shouldn't tell? Yep, it's time for a deep clean. Clear out the bad things, send them to the trash heap, and refuse to bring them back.

Your instructions are clear, Father. Help me get rid of the things that won't help me follow Your quest.

GET READY TO BATTLE

Stop doing the sinful things that are done in the dark. . . . Put on all the things God gives us to fight with for the day.
ROMANS 13:12

This quest to live for God can be a struggle. He gives you the strength you need, and His instructions guide you along the way. Over the last couple of days, you've learned a few things to stay away from. Now? It's time to take the weapons and tools God provides and get ready to do battle.

Refusing to follow God's instructions is like joining the enemy. You can fight for or against God. He doesn't send spies into the enemy camp. He sends courageous and willing soldiers. He supplies them with provisions and gives them the orders they need to stand strong.

Put off old choices and put on new. Put off old habits and put on new. Put off old sin and wrap yourself in the clothes of new life. More instructions are coming on how to do that over the next few days.

Help me put off everything I don't need, God. That way I can put on everything that will help me stand strong.

AVOID THE TRAPS

Be strong with the Lord's strength.
Put on the things God gives you to fight with.
Then you will not fall into the traps of the devil.
EPHESIANS 6:10–11

★

Somehow God does the work, and you get the spiritual muscles. *Nice trade.* But you have to come to Him, knowing that you're weak and in need. If you think you can do it all yourself with your physical muscles, then you miss out on the spiritual strength you need—and that God gives. You'll be fighting with tools that weren't meant for spiritual battle.

If you tell God you don't need the things He provides for battle, then you're a soldier with no tools. You're even telling God that you're smarter than He is, because by refusing what He says you need, you're telling Him He's wrong. God knows there are traps ahead, and His way is the only way for you to avoid them. Trust what He knows.

I don't want anyone to think I'm fighting against You, Father. Your tools are important, and they keep me safe. Help me use what You give me. Help me be a soldier who uses Your strength.

NOT THE ENEMY

Our fight is not with people.
EPHESIANS 6:12

Before you look into the idea of who your enemy is and how to defend yourself in this lifelong quest, there's one bit of very important instruction that needs to sink deep down into your heart, mind, and soul. Let's make this personal: "Your fight is not with people." The enemy is not another boy who picks on you at school, not a brother or sister, and not someone who looks different than you. Your fight will never be with a teacher, coach, or friend. It's not with a neighbor, stranger, or sports rival.

You can't do a good job standing strong against your enemy if you don't know who your enemy is. If your enemy is not other people, then there is no reason to treat anyone like an enemy. The good news is you can stop looking for an enemy where no enemy exists.

My mind can convince me that someone I know is my enemy, Lord. Some people are unkind and can make life hard, but You don't want me to treat them like enemies when they really just need to meet You instead.

KEEP ME STANDING

Our fight. . .is against. . .the spirits of darkness in this world. It is against the demon world that works in the heavens.
EPHESIANS 6:12

★

Today's verse may be hard to understand. You can't see God, but you can see the good things He does. You also can't see the devil, but you can see the damage he does. Both are real and are enemies of each other. Long ago, the devil insisted on becoming God's enemy. He is the only real enemy you have—and he is the same enemy God has.

The devil brings darkness; God brings light. The devil is ruthless; God is kind. The devil wants to destroy; God wants to make things new. The devil doesn't want what God wants, and God doesn't want what the devil wants. And what the devil wants is to destroy people who love God. That's the tough truth about why you need to accept God's help to stand against the enemy.

I'm not standing against a scary movie or a video game, Father. I'm standing against Your enemy, who inspires frightening things. Fear doesn't come from You; it comes from the devil. Protect me from the tricks and traps of the evil one. Keep me standing.

GET DRESSED, GET READY

Put on all the things God gives you to fight with. Then you will be able to stand.
EPHESIANS 6:13

The battle Christians face isn't a fashion show. You don't show up wearing whatever you want to wear. You've been given specific pieces of armor meant to protect you, and it's not practical to wear anything else.

God knows what you need to endure any difficulty, and He prepared these things long before you were born. With His help, you can endure. With His encouragement, you can stand. It is a brave thing to trust God when the battle makes you want to run away. Stay. Stand. Stick close to God with your armor strapped on tight.

Don't leave anything out. Don't swap even one piece of armor for an alternative. It won't work, and it means you've chosen not to follow God's instructions. Put on the things God gives you—never things others give you or things you made yourself.

When I think I know better, remind me of Your instructions, Lord. Let my ears hear, my mind understand, and my actions prove I'm here to stand.

THE IMPORTANCE OF BELIEF

Wear a belt of truth around your body.
EPHESIANS 6:14

If you don't know what to believe, then it will be hard to take action. Most people do what they do because they believe it will help them reach a goal. What you believe is important not just to you but to God. He gave you everything worth believing and then instructed you to believe. Knowing the truth about who God is and who you are as His child can help you stand when things are hard.

People might say you don't know what you're talking about or that you're confused, but the more you know God's truth, the greater your confidence will become.

God's instructions describe truth as a belt. Maybe that's because it ties everything together. It holds everything up. It secures things. Believing a lie, on the other hand, can make you feel unsure. Take God's truth belt—and wear it.

I want to be held together by Your truth, Father. I want to accept that what You say is true so I can stand without hesitation.

A PRIMARY PIECE OF PROTECTION

Wear a piece of iron over your chest
which is being right with God.
EPHESIANS 6:14

★

In the time of knights and lords, armor was essential. It was a foolish soldier who went to war without his armor. God's instructions compare spiritual warfare to physical battles fought by trained soldiers. A soldier would wear a metal chest piece that protected him from arrows shot from enemy bows. An arrow might strike the chest piece, but the construction of the armor prevented it from causing injury.

God says that's what being right with Him does. You stand before the enemy representing the one true God you have chosen to serve. When you wear the chest piece of righteousness—one of the primary pieces of protection you need—God protects your heart from injury.

Being right with God means accepting His truth and obeying His instructions. It means seeking God in prayer and continuing to seek Him by reading His Word. Being right with God means seeing the enemy as wrong and someone you refuse to listen to.

Being right with You should be my everyday goal, Lord. Help me to see righteousness not just as something You want but as something I need.

USE HIS SHOES

Wear shoes on your feet which are the Good News of peace.
EPHESIANS 6:15

There's something satisfying about a good pair of shoes. They can be comfortable, but they can also be supportive. They can cradle your ankles and allow you to move easily without hurting your feet. They let you walk a long way so you can go farther than you could with only bare feet.

God has given you spiritual shoes so you can deliver His message of peace to those who need to hear it. These spiritual shoes give you purpose and provide protection as you take God's message to the places He sends you.

Wear the shoes, accept the protection, and keep walking, because there's no one on earth who doesn't need to know that internal peace is possible. Use His shoes to share the news. And when you stand, trust that your feet are ready to go.

I have so much to learn, Father. You share what I need to know most and then keep sharing. I'll be learning from You for the rest of my life! Help me use Your shoes to take Your message with me everywhere I go.

COVERED BY TRUST

Most important of all, you need a covering of faith in front of you. This is to put out the fire-arrows of the devil.
EPHESIANS 6:16

★

You can call it a shield, a buckler, or a rampart—those are just a few of the names you could use for the "faith covering" in today's verse. Call it what you want, but it's the spiritual proof that you trust God. Trust is something you know is there, and it's something other people notice too.

When the enemy gets mad and sends an arrow to destroy you, the shield will be your trust in God that keeps you safe. You might even see the ways the enemy has tried to harm you, but God keeps protecting you as you keep trusting Him.

God's instructions say that the covering of faith is important. His Word says it is the most important thing you carry with you. Trust in God. Don't trust your skills, experience, or personal bravery. Trust God above all, and never doubt.

I'm thankful I can be covered by trust in You, Lord. You help me stop the arrows that could cause me to doubt You, and You remind me to stand.

DON'T BACK DOWN

The covering for your head is that you have been saved from the punishment of sin.
EPHESIANS 6:17

God corrects. Sin punishes. God wants you to do the right thing, so He guides you in good directions. Sin wants you to fail and punishes you because you failed. Maybe that's why God instructs Christians to stop sinning. He doesn't want to see you punished.

God doesn't condemn His family; instead, He constantly invites you to follow Him. The covering talked about in today's verse is a reminder that you've been rescued. The covering (hat, helmet, cap) is a reminder that God wants you to protect what you think. You've trusted enough to follow. You have faith that keeps you standing. And when the enemy attacks, God wants you to remember all His instructions so you can use your mind to tell every other part of you that now is not the time to back down.

Sin wants to destroy me, Father. It wouldn't be hard to follow sin and find that it accuses me and punishes me in ways You don't. Make me willing to be corrected by You as You protect what I think.

PROTECT AND DEFEND

Take the sword of the Spirit which is the Word of God.
EPHESIANS 6:17

★

If you have heard or read God's truth and accepted it by trusting that it is true, then it just makes sense that you bring God's Word with you as you stand. Others will need to be encouraged, while some will need to hear God's truth for the first time. And the enemy will need to be reminded that he cannot win—and all of that comes from God's Word. *Don't leave it behind.*

The Word of God is one piece of armor that protects *and* defends. Every other piece is used for protection, but the sword of the Spirit takes God's message directly to the enemy. And just like you've read many times in this book, knowing what God has really said is what will help you in moments when you're under fire.

Each piece of your armor is important. You're at risk anytime you leave part of your armor behind.

I need Your help, Lord. You've given me so many ways to accept Your help, and I don't want to reject any of them. When life is hard, help me stand.

GOD'S BETTER ENDING

God makes all things work together for the good of those who love Him and are chosen to be a part of His plan.
ROMANS 8:28

In the middle of your quest, when you look around and notice the struggle you've been through, you may be tempted to give up, step aside, and sit down. But *keep going*.

Today's verse is a reminder that after you've put on every piece of God's armor and used it to take a stand against the enemy, God can take the challenges and hardships you've gone through and use them for your good. He can create something beautiful from something that looked broken and destroyed.

When you stand, you're willing to be part of God's plan. When you follow, you're showing that you love God. When bad things happen, you need to know it's *not* the end of God's story for your life. Keep looking forward to God's much better ending.

I need Your help, Father. I'm not feeling very strong right now. Please give me courage when life gets hard. Thanks for the good You have planned for me. I can't wait to see what You'll do next.

THINGS YOU SHOULD WANT TO DO

Your new life should be full of loving-pity.
You should be kind to others and have no pride.
Be gentle and be willing to wait for others.
COLOSSIANS 3:12

★

Following God not only changes your instructions, it also changes what you choose to do. God's instructions give you a glimpse of the things you should want to do.

"*Your new life should be full of loving-pity.*" Care deeply about people and be ready to help.

"*Be kind to others.*" Don't think it's normal to pick on other people.

"*Have no pride.*" When you see yourself as the most important person in the room, you're forgetting God, who will always be more important.

"*Be gentle.*" Life can be very hard, which is why people often need someone humble to step up and offer a gentle answer.

"*Be willing to wait for others.*" God has always been patient with you. Do the same for others.

After I put on my armor and stand, please help me choose Your better way to treat people, Lord. I want to follow Your example with courage and humility.

BRAIN EXERCISE

Let us keep our minds awake.
1 THESSALONIANS 5:8

★

You sit at a desk in a class at school. You daydream. You internally declare that you're bored. You can't wait until you're an adult so you don't have to think so much. All boys eventually discover something they don't want to learn, can't see why they need to learn it, and decide they would rather be doing something else.

God's instructions say that you should be learning all the time. Keep your mind alert, be willing to read, and be diligent to pray. God's Spirit is your instructor, and He has things to teach; but you won't learn much when you internally declare that you're bored, can't wait until you're an adult so you don't have to think so much, and can't understand why you need to know so much about God.

While you may think you'd rather be doing something else, God says it's important to know what His Spirit is teaching. He wants you to exercise your brain so you can understand and remember His truth.

Keep my mind thinking about You, Father.
Keep me interested in knowing more about You.
Keep me learning, understanding, and growing.

THE LINKS

Be happy with those who are happy.
Be sad with those who are sad.
ROMANS 12:15

★

Pay attention. That's the general instruction in today's verse. If you choose to love other people, then you'll care about the things they're going through. If they're satisfied, join in their satisfaction. If they're struggling, join in their struggle. Happiness links with happiness, and sadness links with sadness. Being a friend links with having friends.

If you make fun of people because they struggle, they won't see you as a very good friend. If you can't be happy for someone with good news, they might not share any more good news with you. God cares enough about you to connect with what you're going through, and He wants you to do the same. That's why He instructed you, "Be happy with those who are happy. Be sad with those who are sad."

Sometimes when I hear about good things happening to others, I'm sad, Lord. But You want me to be happy for them, not sad for myself. Help me be the kind of friend who does the right thing.

THE BIG DEAL

Be happy because you belong to Christ.
PHILIPPIANS 3:1

★

No one made God rescue you. He could have said that He only loved some people, and only those people would be rescued while everyone else was left to figure things out on their own. No, God said He loves *everyone*, and His love is big enough to rescue anyone who asks to be rescued. When you accept His rescue, you can be happy because you gain a new identity. That identity isn't based on what you do but on what Jesus has done for you.

You're rescued because God loves you and you accept His love. Rescue means that you are forgiven of your sins, you have a forever life with God, and you have access to Him whenever you speak His name in prayer.

If this gift seems like no big deal to you, then read today's verse once more: "You belong to Christ." Nothing should stop you from celebrating *that* good news!

When I accept Your rescue, Lord, I'm not only a new person—I'm Your family member! That's incredible news. I want to share it every day because You accept me every day.

THEY TOLD YOU ABOUT JESUS

Remember your leaders who first spoke God's Word to you. Think of how they lived, and trust God as they did.
HEBREWS 13:7

★

Someone introduced you to Jesus. They did a brave thing, and it meant you got a new life and a new opportunity. And now you get to introduce other people to Jesus.

God's instructions for today include remembering the people who told you about Jesus. Maybe it was a friend, your family, or someone at church. Someone had to care about you a whole lot to make the best introduction you've ever known.

That special person should be important to you. You probably pay attention to what they do and what they say. They're an example God used to share His love with you. Spend some time thanking God for the gift of an introduction. But don't stop there. Thank that person for telling you about Jesus. Your encouragement can inspire them to keep sharing God's best news with others.

*When someone talked about Jesus,
I listened, Lord. When they shared good
news, I believed it. When they cared enough
to speak, their courage changed my life.
I'm thankful they talked, shared, and cared.*

TRUTH THAT'S TRUE

"There will be men who will laugh at the truth."
JUDE 18

★

You've read that God is truth. He decides what's true. His Word tells you what's true. What God has said is true can't be changed. You can't vote truth out of the Bible. You can't decide that what God said is mostly true but not completely true. That would mean God lies, and He doesn't.

In today's instruction, you read that some laugh at His truth. They don't want God to tell them what's true. *They* want to decide what's true. When everyone starts to make their own list of what they think is true, then some will want to know who's wrong and who's right. Who should be the final judge of what's true?

Either there is truth that's true no matter what or there is no truth. Truth is what God has given. Even more, truth is who God is! Believe it—don't make fun of it.

I want to pay attention to what You call truth, Father. Help me learn it and believe it. I never want to make fun of it.

BELIEVE; THEN SEE

"First of all, look for the holy nation of God. Be right with Him. All these other things will be given to you also."
MATTHEW 6:33

★

The reason truth is important is that if you don't believe something God has said, then you'll wonder if it's worth believing other things He has said. You might keep questioning whether God means what He says.

If you believe He loves you but you don't believe He can rescue you, then you've missed a very important truth. If He can't rescue, then you're left without any help. The good news is God does love you, He can rescue you, and you do have His help. *That's truth.*

If you believe God can do what He said He would do, then you have to believe He's planning a future home for every member of His family. Your instructions today are to think about this future home anytime you make a decision. As you keep yourself right before God and trust in Him, He makes more gifts available to you. Believe it; then see God work.

Help me trust You enough to believe in the future You've planned for me, Lord. I don't want to doubt Your truth.

A BETTER VIEW

If then you have been raised with Christ,
keep looking for the good things of heaven.
COLOSSIANS 3:1

God brings new life, so the old parts of your life are out of place now. If your life were a puzzle, then the pieces from your old life wouldn't fit with the picture of your new life. If your life were a car, then the parts from the old life wouldn't work with the parts of your new life. If your life were a home, then you'd need to leave the old to make the new your forever home.

Your new life, as one of God's children, enables you to think new things about old problems. You'll love instead of hate, show kindness instead of being rude, and forgive instead of getting back at someone.

When your new life is linked to God's love, you'll think about the good things God has promised. You'll keep seeking His promises; and when you experience His goodness, you'll want to thank Him.

You've instructed me more than once to seek You, Father. I want Your future for me and for all Your people. Keep my eyes watching for Your good plan.

THE INSTRUCTION MANUAL

The Law of the Lord is perfect, giving new strength to the soul. The Law He has made known is sure, making the child-like wise.

PSALM 19:7

★

Every instruction from the Bible is truth because it comes from God's heart. Today's verse says God's Word is perfect. His rules are what give your soul strength. What He has made known, He has made trustworthy. And just like you've read over the past few days, you should keep looking for His truth because God wants to reward your quest with wisdom.

You might buy a toy or a gadget and never read the instructions that come with it. You try to figure out how to play with it on your own, or maybe you've seen someone else play with it, so you think you know what to do. What if that toy will do more than your friend thinks it can? What if it was made to do more than you thought it could?

The Bible is your life quest instruction manual, and it provides all the details of how to make your new life in Christ work for the best.

I can't learn everything from watching others,
and I know I shouldn't just guess, Lord.
Wisdom starts with Your thoughts. Thank You.

IN CONTROL

The Laws of the Lord are right, giving joy to the heart.
PSALM 19:8

Let's say you go to a birthday party, and everything seems a bit crazy. Everyone is doing what they want to do, and no one says, "Stop!" The noise can be a bit overwhelming, right?

Life is a lot like that. A lot of people do whatever they want, while others would just like a little calm. God is not a fan of confusion. That's why He gave rules to follow. When a young person like you follows God's rules, the example you set not only benefits you but also demonstrates for others the difference between control and chaos. The control that shows up when you obey God can lead to joy. How? No one likes feeling out of control. Staying away from chaos provides a sense of peace. Having control over your actions can help you feel safe and bring joy to others.

I want to show self-control in my actions, Father. I want to discover joy because Your rules keep me safe and help me pay attention to You.

GREATER AND MORE FILLING

The Word of the Lord is worth more than gold, even more than much fine gold. They are sweeter than honey, even honey straight from the comb.
PSALM 19:10

Take the most expensive thing you've ever heard about and the food that tastes better than anything else, and neither of them will be as valuable or as sweet as the words God recorded in His book, the Bible.

The things that cost the most can't be your friend, and the best-tasting food will be hard to remember a year from now. God's Word brings life to your everyday dreams and plans. He made you as a one-of-a-kind creation and gives you every reason to live life to the fullest. He says that His Word is greater than riches and more filling than food.

Spending time in God's Word enriches your spirit and sweetens your soul, filling you with the precious thoughts of God Himself. The Bible is the place where weak Christians become strong and hungry Christians are fed. God's Word should never be closed.

I want my spirit to be rich and my soul to be sweet, Lord God. Help me find both in the words You use to instruct me.

ONE BOY STANDING

Watch and keep awake! Stand true to the Lord.
Keep on acting like men and be strong.
1 CORINTHIANS 16:13

★

You are one boy, standing for one God, sharing one message. That message is about the love God has for people who aren't always lovely. Some people have been waiting for the message. Some don't want to hear it. And some want to think about it for a while.

As Christians grow up in their faith, they learn to watch for the enemy, stay awake and on their guard, remain faithful, and trade in their weakness for God's strength.

So if it sounds lonely to be one boy, standing for one God, sharing one message, remember this: God is bringing His family together. Yes, you're one boy standing, but you don't stand alone. Other boys are growing up to trust God too. Other boys are wanting to tell people about Jesus. They could use a friend like you.

I am one boy, and You're my Father. I need Your strength every day, and I would love to meet other kids like me who rely on Your strength too.

FREEDOM

Christ made us free. Stay that way.
GALATIANS 5:1

★

You may not think you're free; but follow Jesus, and you are. You probably should know what freedom is, right? You might think freedom is being able to do whatever you want whenever you want to do it. God made you to be free, so knowing His definition of freedom is important.

God's freedom says you don't have to be bossed around by sin because you're free to say, "No!" God's freedom isn't selfish. It means you're free to do the right thing. You can follow God, help others, and learn from His Word.

You've read about your enemy, the devil, who wants to see you destroyed; but God's freedom means you don't need to believe or cave in to the enemy. God created you to be free from the power of sin. *Stay that way.* You see, God's abundant life is yours when you take God's freedom—and keep taking it.

I can only be free when I follow You, Lord God. I can't say I love You and follow Your enemy. That combination will never work. When I do that, I have no freedom.

IMPORTANT STUFF

Do not fool yourself. If anyone thinks he knows a lot about the things of this world, he had better become a fool. Then he may become wise.
1 CORINTHIANS 3:18

★

You can think you're super smart when, in fact, you're not. Oh, you might know a few things, but what if what you know isn't something God wants you to know? When you think it's important to know things that could lead you to break God's rules, then God says it's time to be willing to become a fool.

In other words, you should be willing to stop learning some things so you can learn more about *God things*. You can't become wise if you keep thinking about unimportant things. Some information can hurt you or people you love (or people you *should* love).

Don't fool yourself by thinking this kind of information is important. It will only take up space in your mind and heart that should be filled with the truth and wisdom found in God's Word.

I want to know what You want me to know, Father. If You don't want me to know something, then I don't want to learn it. Teach me the difference.

RIGHT THINKING

I ask each one of you not to think more of himself than he should think. Instead, think in the right way toward yourself by the faith God has given you.
ROMANS 12:3

★

God wants you to be honest with yourself. Think about who you were without Him and who you are now with Him. He wants you to be honest about how you see other people. They are people God loves, and He wants you to love them too.

You're loved by God. That's really great news. But God loves everybody with the same love, so you should never think you're somehow better than another person or that God loves you more. (Of course, He also doesn't love you less.)

God's instructions say that everyone has broken God's rules, so the only comparison you can make with other people is to agree that people sin. No one is better than anyone else. So stop looking down on others.

I want my thinking to be clear, Lord. Help me think of myself and other people the way You do—not thinking more or less of myself than You think of me. I'm so thankful You love me.

THE ENEMY RUNS AWAY

Give yourselves to God. Stand against the devil and he will run away from you.
JAMES 4:7

★

When you refuse to see yourself the way God sees you and to see others the way God sees them, you may be handing out an invitation to God's enemy, the devil, to talk you out of doing good things and into doing bad things.

On the other hand, when you give God the chance to lead and you agree to follow, then God's enemy has no reason to stay. He'll run away to go pick on someone else. Remember, he doesn't like God, and he doesn't like people who follow God. But no matter how upset God's enemy might be, he will never be stronger or wiser than God. He has to flee when you stand against him in God's strength.

The devil never looks for strength but is happy to find weakness, Father. He doesn't want people to be wise, so he looks for people who make foolish choices. I don't ever want to give him a foothold in my life. Help me to follow You closely so that the enemy runs away.

THE ABSOLUTE BEST EXAMPLE

Be gentle as you care for each other.
1 PETER 5:5

Being sarcastic isn't hard. Some people say sarcasm is a language. When you speak with sarcasm, you're telling someone they did something wrong, aren't very smart, and deserve to be mocked. Does that sound like God's instructions in today's verse?

Ridicule is never required. God doesn't make fun of you or laugh at your mistakes. He offers kindness instead of sarcasm, gentle answers instead of harsh words, and care instead of criticism. God provides the absolute best example to follow.

When you think it's a good idea to make another person feel foolish, remember that God instructs you to be gentle. You might think that being sarcastic with your friends is just what friends do, but the fact that God doesn't treat you that way should motivate you to choose a different response.

Smooth out the rough spots in me, Lord. I don't want to be rude when I talk to other people. I don't want to give them the impression that I think I'm better than they are. Help me to be patient, wise, gentle, and caring.

SOMETHING YOU DON'T DO

"Do not worry about your life. Do not worry about what you are going to eat and drink. Do not worry about what you are going to wear."
MATTHEW 6:25

★

Does God ever give a gift when there's no way to take care of it? Does He forget to take care of the dirt, seeds, water, and sunshine so plants can grow and animals can eat? Has God given you any reason to believe He has given up on His promise to take care of you? The answer to each of these questions is "No!"

You can live without worries. You *should* live with no worries. God's instructions never say, "Worry about these things." The Bible tells you many times that you shouldn't fear, worry, or be anxious. God can take care of everything you worry about, and this same God has never been afraid. He doesn't worry, and nothing comes as a surprise to Him. Trust this fearless leader.

It's no fun to worry, Father, but I find myself worrying too often. If something bothers me, I should bring it to You. Please take care of the things I worry about, and remind me that You're in control.

WORRY KEEPS YOU FROM MOVING FORWARD

"Do not worry about tomorrow. Tomorrow will have its own worries. The troubles we have in a day are enough for one day."
MATTHEW 6:34

When you worry, you can't make good decisions. Take homework, for example. If you worry about doing it right, then you'll struggle to finish. You might somehow believe that not doing the homework is better than doing it wrong.

Worry keeps you from moving forward and causes you to dwell on the worst thing that could happen. If that's true about today, then taking the time to worry about things that *might* happen tomorrow just prevents you from getting anything worthwhile done today.

You can't keep troubles and hardships and challenges from finding you; but even though you can't control any of those things, you can control your response to them. Your best response is to capture your worry and pass it on to God. It's an action that always makes sense.

If I'm going to take action against worry, I want to give it to You, Lord. I don't need it, and You don't want me to have it. Don't let worry keep me from doing what You want me to do.

WORTH BELIEVING

"Follow My teachings and learn from Me. I am gentle and do not have pride. You will have rest for your souls."
MATTHEW 11:29

Jesus didn't say it was a good idea to try out many different options before making the choice to follow Him. He never suggested you should experiment with different ways to live a good life apart from Him. Jesus doesn't offer a plan that allows you to follow Him *some* of the time. In His gentle way, Jesus asks you to watch where He walks and take steps in His direction.

Jesus taught through His words and His actions, and you get to learn from both; but His instructions have never changed. His way is worth following. His truth is worth believing. His life is worth receiving. And when you do, everything is going to be all right. In fact, everything will be better than it has ever been—even when trouble comes. Why? Because you no longer have to face anything alone. Ever.

My life always seems in motion, Father. I have places to go and things to do, but You want my motion to be ever moving in Your direction so that I can learn and grow as I follow You.

THE DIFFERENCE

"Be sure you do not do good things in front of others just to be seen by them."
MATTHEW 6:1

★

Sometimes people try to win a religious popularity contest. They act like they're contestants who want others to vote them "Most Spiritual." They might not really love God but pretend to follow Him because they want you to believe they're better than most people at doing what God wants. But when no one's looking, they stop acting.

Today's instructions are all about doing what God wants you to do because it's the right thing to do and the right time to do it—even if no one sees and no one tells anyone else about your obedience.

When you do good things, other people might notice. Just don't do good things because you want others to notice. There's a difference. God knew there would be a difference, and He gave this instruction so you would understand the difference.

I want to follow You even when no one's looking, Lord God. May my response to You be exactly what You need from me.

FOLLOWING DEPENDS ON THE LEADER

"Be careful that no one leads you the wrong way."
MATTHEW 24:4

★

Your teachers (at school and at home), your coaches, and the crossing guard at school all have the job of helping to lead you in a good and safe direction. They're pretty good at their jobs. But some people have bad ideas about what you should do, where you should go, and whom you should meet.

If you're not following God, then you're headed in the wrong direction (more on that tomorrow). It always makes sense to look for God's wisdom whenever you have a question about what you should do. Guessing is a bad idea because there's a good chance you will be wrong. Besides, if God's wisdom is found in God's Word, you should look for it. If God says He wants you to be wise, you should pray for wisdom. And if God is leading, you should follow Him.

You want me to trust You, Father. If I'm following You, that means I believe You know where You're going and that You're taking me with You. Thank You for leading me on Your path.

THE TWO PATHS

"The door is narrow and the road is hard that leads to life that lasts forever. Few people are finding it."
MATTHEW 7:14

★

God's enemy, the devil, wants as many people to follow him as possible. So this enemy has created an eight-lane expressway that leads to a place called Destruction. He made the path wide because he wants everyone to have an easy time getting into trouble. He made the path smooth and easy so it would seem like a good idea to walk that way. He made it easy to see other people you know walking on the path so it seems like you're in good company.

God's instructions for this quest say that when you want to know God and discover His good plan for you, there is one way in (the door, which represents Jesus), the path is narrow (so you won't wander off), and the road is hard (so you'll learn to rely on God's help and trust His solutions).

Fewer people walk Your path, Lord. But it is the only path that leads to a forever life with You.

EARS HEAR THINGS

"Be careful what you listen to."
MARK 4:24

★

People say some interesting things, don't they? You can find all kinds of quotes by all kinds of people, and often these quotes seem very important. You listen to the things people say; and if the people seem to be smarter than you, you figure you should trust their words. But Jesus said, "Be careful what you listen to."

The truth is, not everything you hear is true. Not everything you read is wisdom. Not everything you trust is trustworthy. If your eyes should be careful what they see, then your ears should be careful what they hear. At the very least, you should learn to ask good questions that will help you determine if the words people say and write match what God actually said. Only those things that line up with the truth of His Word are worthy of your attention.

Give me ears that are tuned to what You have to say, Father. I don't want to pay attention to anything that isn't Your truth.

DON'T TURN OUT THE LIGHT

"Be careful that the light in you is not dark."
LUKE 11:35

Jesus is called the Light of this world (and He says you are too). He came to help people understand God's plan for rescue. A treasure map isn't worth much if you can't read it. God's Word is a treasure that Jesus helped people understand. He still does that today.

Once you begin to understand God's truth, you can help other people understand it too. Jesus' light becomes a light you can shine—and that's just what He wants you to do. He doesn't want you to hide the light or turn it off. You might have the light someone needs to see Jesus as important for the very first time, so let it shine!

Being a Christian shouldn't seem like a secret. Instead, it should seem like the answer to all kinds of problems that people face.

Reflecting Jesus' light is a way I can show care for other people, Lord. So many people have known only the darkness of not understanding the truth, not knowing the source of Your light, and not following You. Thank You for being the God who created light.

WHEN PRIDE SLIPS IN

The person who keeps on sinning is guilty of not obeying the Law of God. For sin is breaking the Law of God.
1 JOHN 3:4

★

This quest you're on leads in a good direction. It can improve your willingness to trust, obey, and love. It can leave you at the top of a spiritual mountain staring down at a valley you don't want to visit just yet. Your faith can inspire you, change the choices you make, and give people a reason to consider joining your quest.

But just when you think you've got everything figured out, it's possible to see pride slip in or almost any other thing that God said is off limits. Then a soldier who knows he is supposed to stand strong might start to break rules without realizing he has stepped off the pathway. If that's you, then you might not recognize that your altered course puts you within sight of Destruction City. That's why God's instructions warn you to keep pride out of your quest.

Help me keep this quest as the adventure of a lifetime, Father. Don't let me walk down the path on my own just because I think I know where I'm going.

A QUEST DELAYED

If you hurt and make it hard for each other,
watch out or you may be destroyed by each other.
GALATIANS 5:15

★

If God's enemy suggests you take a step away from God's path—and then you actually step away—you'll encounter a new danger ahead, and it won't affect just you.

Little changes in your willingness to follow God may mean that you pick on others. Things could become tense at home. You might not get along with other Christians on the path where your quest started.

When you get off the path, you won't agree to work with other Christians to do what God wants done. God wants His people to love each other and work together, but that's hard to do when you're not sure you really want to follow so closely. Because of your wishy-washy attitude, others have trouble trusting you and getting along with you. Then? Nobody remembers to keep their anger in check, say kind words, or pray for wisdom.

Help me want the best for others, Lord.
Help me refuse to fight others on this quest.
The enemy is happy when he can succeed in
stopping the quest for many instead of just one.

JUST DON'T

Be careful that not one of you has a heart so bad that it will not believe and will turn away from the living God.
HEBREWS 3:12

★

You may think people who break the rules are getting away with something. You may think rule breakers are the ones who are free because they do what they want. But something is happening inside a rule breaker.

The truth is, someone who keeps breaking the rules may wish secretly that someone would stop them. They might want to know that someone cares enough about them to challenge their behavior.

A good reason for you to obey shows up in today's instruction. You can break God's rules so much that you refuse to come back to Him and admit He was right. When you break rules and then believe nothing bad has happened or will happen to you, then you might struggle to believe that God is real—and you might even stop looking for Him. Be careful that this doesn't describe you.

If I break a rule, Father, You have time to listen to me. I don't want to wait, put it off, or walk away.

AS IF HE DIDN'T

You must not live any longer like the people of the world who do not know God.
EPHESIANS 4:17

★

God's instructions here are perfectly clear. Don't walk away from God. Instead, walk away from your old life.

You're learning about God; don't act like you're not. This quest is important; don't act like it's not. Following the leader is important; don't act like it's not. When you behave as though God is someone you can take or leave, you are making the same choice that people who don't follow God make.

If God has made a change in your life, then stop behaving as if He hasn't. If He has shown love and you've accepted it, don't pretend it doesn't matter. If God has rescued you, don't act like He didn't have to.

You would expect people who don't know God to act as if He doesn't matter, but you *do* know Him. Be quick to admit that any good change in you is because of God.

Let me give credit where credit is due, Lord God. You've done great things—for me, in me, and through me. People need to know that I think You're awesome.

COME CLOSE

"If My people who are called by My name put away their pride and pray, and look for My face, and turn from their sinful ways, then I will hear from heaven. I will forgive their sin."
2 CHRONICLES 7:14

God told His people, "*Come back to Me.*" This instruction told the people what they needed to do and then it made clear what God would do when they obeyed.

God gives mercy, but He also hates to see His laws broken by people who say they believe in Him, follow Him, and trust His leadership. When Christians act as if God isn't worth much, He doesn't turn away from them but rather encourages them to come back. He's waiting.

In today's instruction, God asks you to put pride behind you and return to Him in prayer. Seek Him by turning away from breaking His rules.

God doesn't say that when you come close to Him, you'll be punished. He says He'll listen. He'll forgive. There's never a good reason to stay away from God.

I never want to be far away from You, Father. Keep me close, show me a better way, and help me follow.

COME BACK AND LEARN

"Call to Me, and I will answer you. And I will show you great and wonderful things which you do not know."
JEREMIAH 33:3

★

In today's verse, God gives more instructions that prove that when you follow God, He agrees to teach you. The quest you're on is not just about moving forward; it's about learning *how* to move forward. It's not just about walking; it's about walking *with* God. It's not just about a journey; it's about where you *end up* at the end of your quest. These are some amazing truths. You might not know them all yet.

There are all kinds of things you don't know and all kinds of things you could learn. Don't recognize God as your teacher but then never attend class. You can't just find out what a class is about and say, "Oh, I've heard about this already." You need to go to class, listen to the instructor, and apply what you've learned by following the instructions.

Thank You for giving me another reminder, Lord. When I walk away, You never want me to stay away. I'm grateful You always welcome me back.

LIFE GIVER

"Get your life from Me and I will live in you. No branch can give fruit by itself. It has to get life from the vine. You are able to give fruit only when you have life from Me."

JOHN 15:4

Life before the quest is only a small part of the story. Your story *really* begins once you join the quest to follow God. That's when you have real life, because then it's in God's hands. His plan and purpose can begin when you agree to walk with Him. Give up a broken past and receive everything you need to grow into something new and useful.

Just like liquid moves through a tree, branch, or vine, and the liquid contains everything the plant needs to grow, a Christian is like a branch attached to the vine. As long as the branch is attached, it will continue to grow and put forth new shoots. You're that branch. You grow because you're attached to the vine—Jesus. What He offers is a wonderful new life.

Choose life. Choose the life giver. Start growing!

I want to grow in my faith, so keep me close to You, Father. I want to be useful, so keep teaching me how.

AN OBEDIENCE PARTY?

"When you do everything you have been told to do, you must say, 'We are not any special servants. We have done only what we should have done.'"
LUKE 17:10

God doesn't ask you to throw a party when you obey. He doesn't want you to declare your own holiday. He doesn't expect you to post anything on social media. He has something different in mind.

His instructions are that Christians should simply point out that they are just doing what needs to be done. They serve God by serving others. They aren't supposed to think of themselves as heroes but rather as those willing to do what God has asked them to do.

Office employees don't ask for applause when they answer the phone because answering the phone is their job. Mechanics don't ask for a parade because they installed a muffler—their employer expects them to carry out that task. You're on a quest, and no doubt God will call you to do some wonderful things. When He does, you can be satisfied knowing that God chose to use you.

Serving You without applause may seem hard, Lord. May I seek to do my best even when no one notices.

TRUTH BLOCKS

Let the teaching of Christ and His words keep on living in you. These make your lives rich and full of wisdom. Keep on teaching and helping each other.
COLOSSIANS 3:16

★

What you've already learned can help you understand something new. Read the Bible, and what you read will help you understand more of God's truth. It's like stacking connecting blocks to build something amazing, but you need to find and use each block to get it done. In the same way, you need to use each biblical learning block to understand God's amazing truth.

Each thing you learn from the Bible is important. God wants you to read and then think about what you read. Take today's instructions, for example. There are truths for you to learn, things for you to do, and instructions for you to follow.

Read today's verse and see if you can find all three. Share what you discover with a trusted adult.

I need to slow down when I read Your Word, Father, so I can think about what it means. Then help me think some more until You've taught me what I need to know for now.

SPEAK IN ONE DIRECTION

Giving thanks and speaking bad words come from the same mouth. My Christian brothers, this is not right!
JAMES 3:10

Who are you when no one is looking? That's worth thinking about, because who you really are might be different than most people think. It could be that you love God but never tell anyone, so they have no idea. Or it could be that you say you love God, but you take very little time to grow your friendship with Him.

Today's instructions suggest that there are some people who say things like "Thank You, God," but then say words that aren't very nice. God says this isn't right. The words you say and the actions you take need to match up with God's instructions. In other words, express your gratitude to God, and don't say words that would hurt others—things God would never say to you. Think about what that looks like and how your choices measure up to God's instructions.

I don't want to be two-faced, Lord, but I can be. My words don't always honor You, and I'm sorry. You're right to ask me to give thanks. With Your help, I can.

DO SOMETHING

Help each other in troubles and problems.
This is the kind of law Christ asks us to obey.
Galatians 6:2

★

You could be an answer to a prayer being prayed by someone you know or perhaps even a complete stranger. God could put you in a place where you do something or say something or use your muscles to move something that helps someone who needs help.

Everyone has problems they want to resolve; everyone has troubles they wish would go away. Some people might be facing a serious struggle, and they don't know how to get through it. You might not know how to help, but God wants you to be willing to help. Sometimes help means listening; and other times, it means doing something.

The Christian quest isn't just about you and God. He has other children, and sometimes He'll ask you to work with Him to help the people He loves as much as He loves you.

Seeing other people the way You see them is important, Father. Please show me the people You want me to help.

KEPT FROM HARM

Children, as Christians, obey your parents.
This is the right thing to do.
EPHESIANS 6:1

★

Obedience is a big deal to God. It means you trust Him enough to do what He asks. It means you believe there's a reason for His instructions. Your quest will be filled with moments when you'll need to do what God asks even when you don't understand why. Today's instructions direct you to obey God by obeying someone else—your parents.

It's true, your parents are not God, and they might even make mistakes along the way, but God still tells you to obey them. Have you ever wondered why? Maybe because when you're young, you need to experience what it's like to follow instructions. You may not remember when you were a toddler, but your parents or other caregivers worked hard to train you not to put things in your mouth that could hurt you, to stay away from danger, and to stop when they told you to stop—all for the purpose of keeping you safe.

Following Your instructions keeps me from harm, Lord. My parents are part of Your plan for my good. Thank You.

A PARENT'S QUEST

"Do your best to teach them to your children. Talk about them when you sit in your house and when you walk on the road and when you lie down and when you get up."
DEUTERONOMY 6:7

★

God's instructions to parents can make things better for you. But for parents to follow these instructions, they'll need to be on their own quest. If they're following God, they can do their best to make sure you continue to learn about God's instructions. They might have been the ones who bought you this book.

Maybe your parents are new Christians and are learning to follow God's instructions just like you are. If they are at the start of their own quest, they'll have to learn to be patient with you, and you'll need to be patient with them.

If you're learning together, take time to talk about God and His instructions whenever you can. Your mom and dad might be able to share things you need to know, and you might be learning things that they need to know.

Give my family opportunities to talk together about You, Father. May we all learn as we share what we know.

NEIGHBORS

"Love your neighbor as yourself."
LEVITICUS 19:18

★

Obedience takes practice. Today's instruction will take work.

You probably avoid doing things that could bring harm to yourself. Instead, you try to protect yourself and take care of your needs. That's normal. What may be a little harder is viewing those around you as people you should protect and take care of.

Do you love other people the same way you love yourself? It's hard at any age, but maybe a little harder when you're a young person. It's easy to think about what you need but hard to pay enough attention to others to know what they need. But paying attention to others is at the very center of today's instruction.

Love will always take time and effort, but that kind of love is exactly what God showed you when He sent Jesus. He must consider you a neighbor!

Neighbors are worth noticing, Lord God. You want me to care for them in the same way I care for myself. You call this kind of care "love." Help me to love others well.

NOT A SUGGESTION

"Serve the Lord your God."
EXODUS 23:25

Don't think of God's instructions as just good suggestions. If you think of them that way, then you could decide you don't need to do what He asks. A suggestion would be something you know God thinks is a good idea, but you get to choose whether you obey. He doesn't give you that option.

You need to understand that if God does the instructing, then He knows your obedience will be good for you. Today's verse directs you to serve the Lord. When you don't serve the Lord but instead serve yourself, then you choose selfishness. The truth is, you *will* serve someone. The person you will be one day might work for money or things. But when you serve God, you have the chance to make an amazing difference in the world that you just couldn't be a part of if you served anything or anyone else.

You keep proving that You're worth serving, Father. Help me go where You send me, follow where You lead me, and love You as You take me there.

NOT FOR SALE

*Keep your lives free from the love of money.
Be happy with what you have. God has said,
"I will never leave you or let you be alone."*
HEBREWS 13:5

★

Boys are competitive and like to show others that they are good at something. It could be sports, video games, or something *you* like to do. One of the things young men eventually get competitive about is money. Most guys want to earn as much money as they can.

Some people devote their whole lives to making money. But God's instructions say that when you love money, you are not loving God as you should. You might like what money can buy, but God offers things you need that are not for sale.

You can lose money and things can be destroyed, but God says His companionship can never be lost or destroyed. Be satisfied with what you have, because when you have God, you'll *always* have enough.

*You will always be more than I need, Lord.
Help me remember that nothing I can buy will
last forever, but what You provide never ends.*

BETTER QUESTIONS

You should want. . .most of all to be able to speak God's Word.
1 CORINTHIANS 14:1

★

If you love God and He's the most important part of your life, then you should want to tell the people you know—and even those you don't know—about Him. That conversation should probably be more than just, "Well, you know, God is cool and stuff." People might want to know why God means so much to you. Can you tell them? Can you explain it? Do you even want to?

Today's instructions clearly indicate that you should want to tell people about God and explain what you know. That's how God's great message reaches people. They need to discover it, and you can help.

Spend some time thinking about how you can share His Good News. What will you need to do to prepare? What will be the most important part of His story to share first? Who gives you the courage to share? Answering these questions will help you be ready.

You want me to tell people there's a way to be rescued from wrong choices and broken lives, Father. Give me the words to say and the courage to say them.

YOU WILL GROW UP

You should want to drink the pure milk which is God's Word so you will grow up.

1 PETER 2:2

★

Maybe you read yesterday's instructions and felt like you were doing something wrong because you don't talk much about God. Just as God gave those instructions, He also gave the instructions in today's verse. Sometimes you just need a little more time to grow up as a Christian. The good news is that you're reading a book filled with God's instructions to help you on your quest. These verses and thoughts are reminders from God about things that are important in your journey.

This book isn't a pep rally or a long motivational speech; it's daily wisdom reminding you that God didn't leave you without instructions for life.

So learn first and then share. Grow up and let God help you make sense of what He says about the importance of His message of love for all humankind.

With You as my teacher, I can learn, Lord. And what I learn from You will always be worth sharing with people who need to know You as much as I do.

A WHISPERED CONNECTION

Come close to God and He will come close to you.
JAMES 4:8

God always stays close to you, but you might not always stay close to Him. If God doesn't seem to be teaching you, it may be that you've just stopped listening. The Bible says that sometimes God speaks in a whisper. That makes sense for a God who is gentle, loving, and kind.

When today's verse says to come close to God and He'll come close to you, it might mean that when you start listening—by reading God's Word to understand what He wants—then you'll start hearing what He's been trying to say to you all along. His instructions will start making sense to you.

For you to understand God, you'll need to stay close and pay attention. Why? God doesn't usually try to reach you through something dramatic like thunder and lightning. He wants a close, quiet relationship with you. He's just waiting for you to want the same thing with Him. Come close—and listen.

You found me first, and now You want me to seek You, Father. I want to get to know You better, love You more, and share You often.

CLEAN THE JUNK ROOM

Clean up your hearts, you who want to follow the sinful ways of the world and God at the same time.

James 4:8

★

A lot of people have a special room in their house where they put all the things they don't know what to do with. Using this room as a storage space is easier than trying to clean it.

God's instructions show that your heart can have the same type of room; but instead of keeping extra clothes, broken vacuums, or old exercise equipment in it, you store sin you don't want to tell God about. You store plans that don't include God. This heart-room might even contain a few things you're hanging onto from your old life. Just outside that room, you post a Keep Out sign and don't give God full access to your heart.

Invite God in to help you clean things up. . .and all distractions can go away.

That place in my life that I thought I could hide from You is something I need help with, Lord. Help me get rid of everything that's slowing down my growing up.

COMFORT AND STRENGTH

Comfort each other and make each other strong.
1 THESSALONIANS 5:11

★

God has always wanted you to think about other people. That's why He instructs you to help those in need. They include neighbors, strangers, friends, and family. He wants your compassion for other people to look just like His compassion for you. When you learn about God's kindness, it's something you can show others every day.

Today's verse mentions things you are asked to do for other Christians. These instructions were written to believers who attended the church at Thessalonica in the Bible, but they are instructions you can follow too. Trouble comes to visit everyone from time to time (including Christians), so when you see a Christian friend struggle, comfort them and remind them that God gives strength to people who are struggling. What a great reminder! God also sends good friends like you to help.

Thinking of what I need is easy to do, Father. But seeing other people in need sometimes makes me uncomfortable, or I look the other way because I assume someone else will help. Please help me help others.

THE TROUBLE PROMISE

"In the world you will have much trouble.
But take hope! I have power over the world!"
JOHN 16:33

Jesus never promised that becoming a Christian would make your life easy. Life with Jesus is always much better than life without Jesus, but His instructions say you can expect to experience trouble—and perhaps a lot of it. If you wonder why you should follow God and His Son if all you can expect is trouble, you should know that there will be trouble without God too. The biggest difference is that when you're on a quest with God, you have His help. And if you're wondering why that's important, remember Jesus' final words in today's verse: "I have power over the world!" Having His power is much better than trying to live life without His help.

There are benefits to going through struggle, and you'll read more about them in the next few days. Yes, trouble and hardship will show up, but many good things come from bad days.

When I have bad days, it's good to know I'm not the only one, Lord. Thanks for letting me know trouble would come. Please teach me how to endure.

A COMFORT OBSERVED

He gives us comfort in all our troubles. Then we can comfort other people who have the same troubles. We give the same kind of comfort God gives us.
2 CORINTHIANS 1:4

★

You can learn so many things from God. When you do, God wants you to make sure others can see what you've learned. When you struggle and God shows up to help, you'll see what that looks like and feels like, and you'll realize why it's important to show up to help other people in their troubles. When He calms you down and comforts a crushed heart, you know that others will need to experience the same help. What God gives you isn't something you should keep to yourself.

Your quest will be filled with the struggles of an epic journey, but you have a destination to look forward to, a path to walk on, and a God who has promised to help.

You're there for me when I hurt the most, Father. Because You help me, please help me be there for others when they struggle. This quest is for many, and You ask us to help each other.

GOOD OUTCOMES

Troubles help us learn not to give up. When we have learned not to give up, it shows we have stood the test. When we have stood the test, it gives us hope.

ROMANS 5:3–4

★

When a cowboy breaks a horse, he takes what the horse views as trouble to make the horse useful. The horse doesn't start life knowing what it's like to have a rider. When you break a horse, you're teaching it to recognize a companion and to follow certain instructions that will make things easier.

You don't start life knowing how to face trouble. It can seem super frightening when you experience it, but God teaches you how to recognize that He is with you and shows you that His instructions will make things easier if you follow them. Don't give up. Stand the test. Discover that you trust God's ability to help. That chain of events will always start with trouble, but a good outcome is waiting.

When You start to help me, I don't want to resist, Lord. It may seem confusing, but Your help is what I need even when I don't think what You're doing is helping.

BAD THINGS MADE GOOD

The man who does not give up when tests come is happy. After the test is over, he will receive the crown of life. God has promised this to those who love Him.

JAMES 1:12

★

Today you get to explore one of those good outcomes you read about yesterday. It's important to do more than say that God can make bad things good—especially if you're waiting for a good ending.

Sometimes you can't see the good right away. You need to talk to God, think about what happened, consider what you learned, and then discover something good that you never expected.

Today's instructions say that any sadness you feel now will be replaced with joy, because while tests come and go, your life with God is forever. Think about this next verse. It's not an instruction, but a promise about this good outcome: "The little troubles we suffer now for a short time are making us ready for the great things God is going to give us forever" (2 Corinthians 4:17).

I'll need to be patient while I wait for Your good outcome, Father. Thanks for the reminder that a good outcome is on the way.

GET RID OF IT

Let us put every thing out of our lives that keeps us from doing what we should. Let us keep running in the race that God has planned for us.
HEBREWS 12:1

★

You're a boy on an adventure. Make sure to travel lightly. Don't carry things you don't need. You won't need anything that looks like anger or unforgiveness, so leave them behind. You won't need bad thoughts, selfishness, or rude language. You don't need to take memories of the mean things people have done to you. If anything keeps you from your quest, get rid of it! If there's something you know God wants you to do, but you're carrying something else that won't let you do what He asks, then it's time to get rid of whatever slows you down and stops you from following God's instructions.

It will be easier to finish your quest without baggage you don't need and that God doesn't want you to have.

You give me what I need for my journey, Lord God. You ask me to leave behind what You don't give. Thanks for walking with me. My life is so much better with Your help.

IN THE WAITING

They who wait upon the Lord will get new strength. They will rise up with wings like eagles. They will run and not get tired. They will walk and not become weak.
ISAIAH 40:31

★

God knows what He will do, and He knows when He will do it. Your requests are never forgotten or ignored. When you pray, God knows the exact time to give you what you need. When you trust God in this time of waiting, some pretty cool things can happen.

You won't have to worry because God promises to answer. You can move forward because God walks with you. You don't have to grow weary because God takes care of you. And you don't have to stay weak because God gives you strength.

Your instructions today are to trust God and then watch Him transform bad things into good things.

You're worth trusting, Father. Your plans are good, Your timing is perfect, and Your strength is exactly what I need. Thank You for giving me everything I need to follow where You lead.

DON'T TRUST THE WRONG THING

Trust in the Lord with all your heart, and do not trust in your own understanding. Agree with Him in all your ways, and He will make your paths straight.

PROVERBS 3:5–6

★

You can come up with all kinds of reasons for why you need what you think you need and why you need it now. You might even try to convince God that He should give you what you want. This game plan means you *will* waste time doing something that changes nothing.

God knows more than you do, and He knows what you really need and what's best for you. If you trust your heart, then today's instructions say you're trusting the wrong thing. Trust God. Agree with Him that He has the best ideas, and then watch Him make complicated things simpler.

You don't have all the answers to every question. That's why it makes sense to trust the God who knows the answers to questions you haven't even thought to ask.

I want to trust You with all my heart, Lord. When I ask for Your help, make me brave enough and patient enough to wait for Your good answer.

STAND FOR GOD

Fight the good fight of faith.
Take hold of the life that lasts forever.
1 TIMOTHY 6:12

It will seem easier to refuse to trust God than to keep believing—but keep believing. When things get tough, it will seem logical to stop and hide until things get easier—but keep standing. You might even be tempted to say that God isn't so important, but you know something different. Don't you?

There's a life that pays no attention to polls and popularity. It is a life where only God's opinion counts. This is the life you get to live every day, if you so choose. It may not feel good when people disagree with you, argue with you, or tell you that you're wrong. That's why faith is described as a fight. The life of faith is not easy, but its benefits are eternal.

Faith in God is a big decision, and it changes your everyday choices. And then what happens? Your future changes. The gift of life that lasts forever is worth the discomfort of going against the flow and standing for what you know is right.

I never want to say I don't know You, Father.
Help me remember all the good gifts
You've given me. I want to stand for You.
Please help me do what seems hard.

NO TROUBLEMAKERS

Be at peace with all men.
Live a holy life. No one will see the Lord without having that kind of life.
HEBREWS 12:14

No one likes a troublemaker. They're good at making people mad. Sometimes they create conflict by pitting people against each other. Troublemakers are good at saying the very thing that can convince you to make choices you wouldn't usually make. God's instructions? Don't be a troublemaker. Get along with people. Let God use you to make life better for others.

When you cause trouble for other people, you're not showing love, and love is God's most important instruction. If you choose trouble, you will struggle to recognize God. Sure, He's there, but you might not notice Him because nothing you're doing matches His instructions.

Choose now, today, this very moment, to make a change that follows God's instructions away from trouble and toward Him. He has always wanted you to be set apart from troublemakers.

If You don't want me to be a troublemaker, then I don't want to be one, Lord. Help me choose peace so You can use me—and so I can be close to You.

THE FORGIVEN FORGIVE

Forgive other people just as God forgave you because of Christ's death on the cross.
EPHESIANS 4:32

★

You probably know that forgiveness is something God wants you to show, but what is forgiveness? You know God has forgiven you, but what exactly did He do for you? Did He say that the laws you broke weren't important? No. He has clearly said that breaking His rules puts distance between you and God.

Forgiveness is your choice to offer to God your feelings of anger and sadness over something that wasn't your fault. It doesn't try to repay the bad choice of another with a bad choice of your own. It's a gift to others that they don't deserve—and they don't have to repay. Forgiveness doesn't mean you forget the pain the other person caused, nor does it mean you suddenly believe that what they did was right or was no big deal. Forgiveness simply means you refuse to allow the poor choice of someone else to change the direction you're headed.

I'm on a quest, Father. I don't want to be sidetracked or abandon the journey. You forgave me. Please help me make the same choice to forgive others.

LOVE BEATS FEAR

Grow in the loving-favor that Christ gives you. Learn to know our Lord Jesus Christ better. He is the One Who saves.

2 PETER 3:18

★

Something changes inside you when you're loved. Hard places deep inside become soft. Uncertainty makes room for trust. Angry words come face-to-face with calm answers. When you don't know love, you're afraid. You might be afraid of how people will act, afraid that no one can be trusted, or afraid that your bravest hope is a bad idea.

God loves you; and like fertile soil that grows healthy plants, His love is the one thing that can make you grow. Choose His love, learn His instructions, and remember that He rescues people who understand they're lost.

Choose God, and you get love in return. That love has always been waiting for you. It is love that rescued you, and it is love (not fear) that keeps you close to God. Grow and keep growing. Receive love and love others. Be rescued and share the Good News—God rescues.

Your love does something amazing, Lord. Help me accept Your love. Make me willing to share it.

BEEN SIN FOOLED?

Help each other. Speak day after day to each other while it is still today so your heart will not become hard by being fooled by sin.
HEBREWS 3:13

★

You need people to encourage you, and they need you to return the favor. Even if they don't start the encouragement, you can start it—and you should keep encouraging. You can help them and then do it again tomorrow. You can pray for them and remember them every time you pray.

God's instructions direct you to encourage others "day after day." It's not something you do once and then say, "My work here is done." No, your encouragement is just beginning.

Everyone has been fooled by sin. It convinces you that nothing is wrong with doing the wrong thing. Sin might say that you probably won't get caught, that God isn't being fair, or that you really should have exactly what you want.

When you receive regular encouragement and help, you're more likely to remember that sin always lies.

I need encouragement, Father. Thank You for encouraging me. Give me opportunities to encourage others. And maybe someone will encourage me too!

NEVER ON YOUR OWN

Let yourself be brought low before the Lord.
Then He will lift you up and help you.
JAMES 4:10

The choices you've made haven't always been good. God said you would sin, and you have. You try to do your best, but you're pretty certain your best isn't good enough for God. You may feel defeated and maybe even sad. That's when you come to God and say, "I can't do this on my own. I made the choice to do the wrong thing even when I was certain I didn't want to."

That sounds like a horrible place to be, but what if it's just where you need to be? If that sounds strange, then read today's instructions once more. When you are at low points in your life, you shouldn't simply try harder or, worse yet, turn away from God. He wants you to come to Him so He can pick you up, encourage you, and help you do things (like obey, love, and forgive) you can't do on your own.

I am weak and You are strong, Lord God. You can do what I never could. Please do the impossible in me.

TELL THE RIGHT STORY

See that no one misses God's loving-favor. Do not let wrong thoughts about others get started among you. If you do, many people will be turned to a life of sin.
HEBREWS 12:15

★

God said that He is the way you define love. His kindness gives people a reason to learn more about Him. You can show people the love of the one-of-a-kind God. Or you can make it hard for them to see His love by pointing out all the things they are doing wrong. You can spend time telling others all you've learned about the bad things certain people have done. That's called gossip, and God doesn't want it showing up in your life.

Today's instructions say that when you don't tell God's story correctly, and when you fail to show His love, you're pushing people in the direction of sin. Your poor representation of God and His love can influence not just people who don't know Jesus, but even other Christians. Be careful to represent God well and tell His story with love.

You are so loving, Father. Help me point to Your kindness first. People need to know who You are.

A GIFT JUST FOR YOU

God has given each of you a gift. Use it to help each other. This will show God's loving-favor.

1 PETER 4:10

You have a gift that God designed just for you. You might not recognize it yet, but it's there and it's yours. This gift can be used to help others, so keep it *and* give it away. God's gifts should never be used to destroy. If His gift is love, then you shouldn't hate. If His gift is kindness, you shouldn't be rude. If His gift is peace, you shouldn't be a troublemaker. He has given you all three of those gifts, and more are available for you to share with others.

You've been instructed—so use God's good gifts to do good things. Represent God so well that when people see your actions, they can also see themselves knowing God—the One you honor through the way you use His gifts. He's also the One who loved you enough to be the first to share.

Help me discover the gifts You've given me, Lord. Let me be willing to share them with others. Give me a life that looks more and more like You every day.

NOT THE ONLY CHOICE

Do not let sin have power over you.
Let good have power over sin!
ROMANS 12:21

There's a good reason you shouldn't ignore sin. It doesn't know when to stop, slow down, or give you a break. It's like telling a bully they're free to bully you anytime they want. Sin wants to take control; and you give it the launch codes for personal destruction when you act like it doesn't exist, isn't a problem, and never was a big deal.

The instructions in today's verse give a better option. Because God is good, you should let *Him* have power over sin in your life. When He helps, you can say no to sinful choices. He can offer a way out when you think sin is the only choice you have.

Remember that sin wants you to believe you have no choice. God's goodness says you *always* have a choice. God's goodness tells you the truth about what you can choose to do.

I don't want to sin and keep sinning, Father.
I want to do good and keep doing good. Please help me.

DON'T FOLLOW THE WRONG LEADER

My son, if sinners try to lead you into sin, do not go with them.
PROVERBS 1:10

As bad as sin is, it also asks others to join it in trying to stop you from following God. Those who make the choice to sin are bullied by sin—because sin doesn't want just one person to follow.

God wants to put together a team of boys like you so His goodness can be found in all kinds of places. But sin also wants a team. Your bad choice can mean that others also want to make bad choices. And sin doesn't like to release its players.

Don't follow sin. Don't become a member of its team. You don't even need to sit in the stands and watch what happens when people sin.

A day is coming when a bad leader will try to get you to follow him. Don't fall for his plans. Heed today's instructions and refuse to walk with sin.

Because I don't want to follow sin, could You help me follow You, Lord? Sin demands I follow, but You have a better path. Keep walking with me on this good quest.

LIVE A NEW LIFE

Think of yourselves as dead to the power of sin. But now you have new life because of Jesus Christ our Lord. You are living this new life for God.
ROMANS 6:11

★

Today's Bible instructions say that sin doesn't have power over you anymore. It's possible you're thinking, *If that's true, then why do I still break God's rules?* That's a very good question.

God said you should think of yourself as dead to the power of sin, but how can you do that? This verse almost sounds as if sin can't touch you and you'll never sin again. Is that what it means?

God has defeated sin, and He has the power to help you make choices that lead toward your best life and away from sin. But *you* must link your choices to God's instructions. You have to ask for God's help, because without it, you'll never have enough of your own power to avoid sin.

You're less likely to sin when you spend time living a new life *for* and *with* God.

I want Your power to make good choices, Father. I want Your power to help and not sin's power to hurt.

THE WAY YOU SPEND TIME

Make the best use of your time. These are sinful days.
EPHESIANS 5:16

★

Have you ever really paid attention to how you spend time? It's easy to waste time. It's harder to use it for good. There are so many ways to spend time, but spending time following God's instructions is a perfect way to use the time God gives you. And then. . .spend a little more time *doing* what He says you should do.

It isn't very wise to think that you can do what God says you should, but only if you can do it later—sometime in the future. Anyone can do that, and it's easy to keep pushing obedience to a later date on your calendar. After a while, you'll probably forget your good intentions altogether.

Sin is common, and it's a huge time waster. Using time wisely is a great way to sin less often.

If I'm spending time doing what You want me to do, Lord, then I won't have much time to even think about sinning. Because sin is so common, help me spend time thinking about ways I can obey You.

MORE THAN BEING NICE

When someone does something bad to you, do not do the same thing to him. When someone talks about you, do not talk about him.

1 PETER 3:9

Sometimes boys need specifics. That's what instructions do, right? They provide specific guidelines on a topic. Then you don't have any excuse to break the rules, because the rules are clear.

The instruction could have been "Be nice." But then you might wonder who you need to be nice to. You might think there are some people you should be nice to, while others don't matter quite so much. God knows you might be tempted to think this way, so He made sure you would know that even when someone isn't nice to you, you should still be nice to them. Or when someone says rude things about you, you should still be nice to them.

Don't accept the idea that you should pay people back for what they do to you. God says you should give people good things that they might not deserve.

You ask me to do for others what You've already done for me, Father. I want to remember what it feels like to receive mercy and grace.

GOD DOES GOOD THINGS BETTER

Instead, pray that good will come to him.
You were called to do this so you might
receive good things from God.
1 PETER 3:9

★

Today's instructions wrap up what you read about yesterday. Even when people say mean words or do rude things, you should do good things for them. The verse continues with something that may seem strange. More than just being nice to someone who is mean, you are instructed to ask God to do good things for a mean person. That's not easy for someone who has been picked on, let down, or left out.

You might find the last part of today's verse interesting. It says that doing good things for people who refuse to do good things for you means that, instead of waiting for *them* to do good things for you, you can be assured that *God* will do good things for you. And God does good things better than any human ever could.

I want to always remember that You don't ask me to do things to make life hard, Lord God. You ask me to obey, and then You bless me even when others don't.

WHY YOU BELIEVE

Always be ready to tell everyone who asks you why you believe as you do. Be gentle as you speak and show respect.
1 PETER 3:15

★

When mean people see that you repay their bad actions with good actions, they might ask you why you would do that. This is where all of God's quest instructions will make perfect sense. When you know that what you believe is how you live, you can share the truth of what God can do in a life that accepts His help.

First, you'll need to know what you believe and why you believe it. You can't really help anyone understand what God is doing when you're not sure yourself. Don't get defensive; show respect, and tell the truth about God's love and the difference He has made in your life. Share the freedom you've found in following His instructions. Let those instructions inspire you to obey.

People might not care whether they get to know You if they can't see that You change lives, Father. Make me willing to tell people how You've changed me. Use my life to draw others to You.

THE GIFT GOD WANTS

Give your bodies to God because of His loving-kindness to us. Let your bodies be a living and holy gift given to God. He is pleased with this kind of gift. This is the true worship that you should give Him.

ROMANS 12:1

God wants a gift. Will you give it to Him? This gift includes your hands and feet, your heart and mind, your hopes and dreams. The gift comes in one package—your *body*. Your body is something God can use to help other people. After all, if God wants you to go help someone, you need your body to do that. Giving your body to Him as a gift means you're willing to help.

God didn't just ask for your eyes, your mouth, your heart, your brain, or your hands. He wants *everything*. A gift of your body tells God that serving Him in the way you walk, talk, and act is the perfect way to say, "Thank You."

I want to give You every part of me, Lord, and I don't want to take back what I give to You.

LOOK FORWARD TO HEAVEN

Keep your minds thinking about things in heaven. Do not think about things on the earth.
COLOSSIANS 3:2

★

Think about heaven because God is there. Think about heaven because you'll meet Him there. Think about heaven because there will be no pain or sadness there. *Think. About. Heaven.*

Heaven is a forever place. It's not like history that has a beginning and an end. Even if you live to be one hundred years old, you won't experience anything here (apart from the day of your rescue) that will be as perfect as what you will experience in heaven.

Earth exists so you have a time and place to decide about who Jesus is and whether you'll accept His rescue. Heaven exists for those who've said yes to rescue. That's why spending all your time thinking of what you get to do here falls short of God's instructions for you. You can appreciate the beauty God created here on earth, but always look forward to heaven. It will exceed your greatest hopes and dreams.

I'm curious about everything that awaits Your people in heaven, Father. Help me look forward to my future home with You. With You is where I belong.

THE EXAMPLE

Show them how to live by your life.
TITUS 2:7

People are watching how you live. *They really are.* If you say you're a Christian, then people want to see the difference between the way you live and the choices they make. Kids younger than you will look up to you to see how they might want to live. What do they see?

Second Corinthians 5:20 says that you represent Jesus. He wants people to see Him when they look at you.

God gives His followers instructions. Do people see obedience to those instructions in what you do? They should. Today's verse directs you to show others how to live by your example. You have an example in Jesus; and when others see your example, they just might be inspired to put their trust in Jesus too.

Today's instructions mean that you have a responsibility to do *more* than just think God is awesome—because people are watching. Be an example.

You want me to be an example, Lord. I want that too. I want my choices to line up with Your instructions.

HELPFUL WORDS AND FOOLISH TALK

Do not listen to foolish talk about things that mean nothing. It only leads people farther away from God.
2 TIMOTHY 2:16

★

People say things—a lot of things. Sometimes words can be helpful, but sometimes what you hear will hurt. Other words might not hurt, but they aren't helpful either. What you should want to hear are helpful words. Be careful to sift out foolish and meaningless words from all the talk in your life.

One easy way to follow today's instructions is to ask if the words you're listening to are helpful. If they're instructions from a parent, the answer is yes. But if they're unkind words said about someone you know, they likely qualify as "foolish talk."

You might hear some people talk disrespectfully about God, saying things about Him that you know aren't true. Those kinds of words won't lead you closer to God—and closer to Him is what you need.

I can choose the words I listen to, Father.
I can choose the words I share with others.
May the words I say be pleasing to You.

DOING IT RIGHT

Do your best to know that God is pleased with you. Be as a workman who has nothing to be ashamed of. Teach the words of truth in the right way.
2 TIMOTHY 2:15

The best kinds of jobs are those for which you're specifically trained. There's no guessing, and you're free to do the work without wondering if you're doing it right. Why? Someone trained you—and you learned how to do it right.

But jobs can be hard if you're not trained but simply expected to know what to do. You can get into trouble doing this kind of job, because even though you want to do the right thing, you probably don't know how.

As a Christian, you have a special job to do. The work you do for the Lord doesn't need to be hard, because God gives you the instructions you need. You can do what He asks and never have to be ashamed, because you've learned to follow His instructions.

I have read more than 150 of Your instructions, Lord God. Help me remember them. Help me follow them. Thank You!

WHEN YOU'RE NOT SURE

Keep away from everything that even looks like sin.
1 THESSALONIANS 5:22

★

Sometimes people who want to follow God will think that what He really means by *obedience* is that people can get as close to breaking His rules as they want so long as they don't "actually" break them. Today's instructions offer a different idea.

Instead of seeing what you can get away with, you should stay away from things that even look like they *might* break His rules.

Sometimes boys get into trouble and parents hope they learn from their mistakes; but a wise God wants you to know that if something sounds like you shouldn't do it, then you shouldn't do it.

Keep learning every day, and if you don't know whether something is right or wrong—but you think it *might* be wrong—then avoid it for now. This instruction helps protect you, and it sends a good message to those who watch you live your faith.

I don't want to break Your rules, Father, even if I don't do it on purpose. May I be willing to say no to something when I'm not sure You would want me to do it.

MOVED IN GOOD DIRECTIONS

"Ask, and what you are asking for will be given to you. Look, and what you are looking for you will find. Knock, and the door you are knocking on will be opened to you."
MATTHEW 7:7

★

You've already read that God is never confused, but you can be. He has a plan, even when yours isn't working. He wants good things for you at the very same moment you break His rules.

Ask Him for help, look for His answers, and check for proof that He's leading you.

Today's quest instructions are a great reminder that God wants to be involved in your life. He wants to help you make good decisions. His plans move you in a good direction. There's no reason to walk His path without help, no reason to guess what He's asking, and no reason to stop your quest because you don't know what to do next. He has answers, and He doesn't want you to waste time guessing.

You want me to ask for help, Lord God, so I'm asking. You want me to look for Your answers. Please show me. Lead me and help me know when You're leading.

MERCY TO YOU

"You must have loving-kindness just as your Father has loving-kindness."
LUKE 6:36

★

When someone breaks the law, they might get a fine, spend time serving their community, or maybe even spend some time in jail. Breaking the law can have severe consequences. God made the very first set of laws, and He doesn't want you to break those laws either.

Justice says anyone who breaks the law must be punished by getting exactly what they deserve. Mercy, or loving-kindness, is the way God prefers to deal with people who break His laws—*people like you*. Mercy says, "You will *not* get what you deserve."

It's interesting that people who want justice don't like mercy very much, but those who have received mercy often think a lot about their need to obey God's laws. That's because mercy proves a relationship between you and God, while justice marks a growing distance between people and God. Show mercy because God has shown mercy to you.

I'm grateful when You show mercy to me, Father, but I'm not always happy to see mercy given to people I don't think deserve it. Your mercy is what You ask me to give others. Please help me!

PROMOTING PEACE

Live in peace with each other.
1 THESSALONIANS 5:13

Mercy promotes peace because it makes friendships stronger. Justice also can make peace possible, but the lessons are harder. Mercy is like a grandma asking a child who has broken the rules to come sit with her while she offers advice and comfort. Justice is like a school principal who calls parents because a wrong choice was made. God can use both mercy and justice to bring peace. Sometimes justice is the only answer, but God most often starts with mercy—and *you should too*.

The rules God asks you to follow lead to peace. When people don't follow the rules, peace is hard to find. Peace can grow only when people believe that God made the rules and then choose to obey them.

You should know that God's peace is something that happens inside you but is not always something that happens in the world around you. When bad things are taking place around you, you can still be at peace on the inside if you follow God's quest instructions.

You want me to seek peace with others, Lord. Use mercy when You can and justice when You need to so that I can live with Your peace.

THE PERFECT EXAMPLE

Do as God would do. Much-loved children want to do as their fathers do.
EPHESIANS 5:1

This book is filled with instructions from a God who sets a great example for you to follow. He doesn't finish His list of instructions by saying, "*Pay no attention to what I do—just get out there and do everything I said.*" Humans might say something like that, but God wants you to *follow His example*. He's asking you to do the very same things He already does.

There isn't one set of rules that God follows and another set you should follow. There is just one—it's the same set of rules. The difference is that only God follows His own rules every single time.

It's always easier to follow someone's example when they show you what to do by doing it themselves. That's the kind of example God is to you and the kind of example He wants you to be for others.

Thanks for being my best example, Father. Thank You for showing me that You won't ask me to do something that You won't do. I have no excuse not to follow You.

SHARE IT OFTEN

Preach the Word of God. Preach it when it is easy and people want to listen and when it is hard and people do not want to listen. Preach it all the time.

2 Timothy 4:2

★

You've read instructions that tell you to share what you know with people you meet. This set of instructions repeats something you've already read, but then it adds something more.

God's news is worth sharing even when people don't seem to be interested in listening. When God gives you instructions, you are not responsible for making sure the outcome is good. That's God's job (remember, He said He can take bad things and make them good). He just wants you to follow His instructions and share them. Sometimes people who don't seem to be listening really are listening. God can use your words to deliver His message.

I want to share even when it's hard and even when people won't listen, Lord. Even when people think they don't want to hear the truth, everyone needs to hear Your Good News. Help me take it with me everywhere I go and share it often.

DO IT YOURSELF?

A man cannot please God unless he has faith. Anyone who comes to God must believe that He is. That one must also know that God gives what is promised to the one who keeps on looking for Him.

HEBREWS 11:6

Your quest is important, but it's meaningless if you don't have faith. Faith is absolute trust in God, His plan, and His rescue. Looking for Him is part of the adventure.

Maybe you're trying to walk in God's direction without any guidance or help. Maybe you're trying to reach Him on your own—which is just not possible. You might consider yourself better than others, more dedicated than some, and more sincere than anyone; yet, if you're trying to live a good life apart from faith, you're still lost and in desperate need of rescue and forgiveness for breaking God's rules.

Your quest is not a do-it-yourself project. It isn't even a *doing-your-best* project. When you try to make the adventure all about you, you leave out the most important part of the quest—God Himself.

I don't want to act like a Christian; I want to be one, Father. If I'm going Your direction, then let me follow You.

PRETENDERS

"You who pretend to be someone you are not, first take the big piece of wood out of your own eye. Then you can see better to take the small piece of wood out of your brother's eye."

MATTHEW 7:5

★

Some people pretend to be Christians but think they can rescue themselves. God's instructions say that's not how rescue happens. Today's instructions are for people who think they can speak for God when it comes to deciding how good or bad someone else is.

These people are called pretenders. God isn't a fan. This kind of person wants to tell anyone willing to listen about people who break God's rules. They want to name every broken law. They want to shout the word "Guilty!"

But today's instructions, spoken by Jesus, say that it's better to think about the rules you've broken and to deal with your own sins before you ever start taking the sins of other people to ears willing to hear your list.

I don't know more than You, Lord, and I'm not any better than other people. Help me remember that You can take care of mercy and grace and discipline. You've asked me to love.

THROUGH YOU

Comfort those who feel they cannot keep going on. Help the weak. Understand and be willing to wait for all men.
1 THESSALONIANS 5:14

★

If God doesn't want people trying to reach Him on their own and He doesn't want pretenders, then what instructions does He have for boys who want to follow God and love people?

Today's verse may give a good answer. God has helped you in the past, continues to help you today, and always will help you. He understands you and has been waiting patiently for you your entire life. He offers compassion and comfort. He recognizes your weaknesses and loves you no matter what.

Now? Do the same for others. That's His instruction. Will you do it? Help others—and don't stop. Work to understand them—and be willing to wait. Be patient and kind. Recognize that people get weak and need God's compassionate love—through you.

These are great instructions for the adventure of a lifetime.

Help me be this kind of Christian, Father. The kind who shows compassion and not an eagerness to gossip. I don't want to pretend to follow You. I want to find Your steps and walk in them.

LET GOD HELP YOU

"Think how the flowers grow. They do not work or make cloth. Yet, I tell you, that King Solomon in all his greatness was not dressed as well as one of these flowers."
LUKE 12:27

When was the last time you saw a bird knit a sweater or go to the grocery store to buy supplies for a mealworm casserole? When was the last time you saw a flower go online to put in an order for water or fertilizer? You haven't because birds don't knit and flowers don't have web access.

Pretenders worry about a lot of things because they're never sure if they are doing anything right. Do-it-yourselfers can only follow their own plans. Christians, on the other hand, know that if God takes care of birds and flowers, they don't need to worry, because what they can't take care of, God can. The things God takes care of are in better shape than the best-dressed kid in class. Your instructions? Let God help you—and stop worrying.

I can think of all the things I need, Lord. Help me remember all the things You've given me.

A TIME TO TURN AWAY

Turn away from the sinful things young people want to do. Go after what is right. Have a desire for faith and love and peace.
2 TIMOTHY 2:22

If you do what everyone else does, but what everyone else does isn't what God wants you to do, then it's time to turn and run away from bad choices.

Sin is an easy choice because you just have to think about yourself. What do you want? How do you feel? When do you want something? When you can't think of others and when you won't think about God, you'll make choices that are "sinful things young people want to do."

God's instructions are simple: "Go after what is right." That's a little harder because it means you'll need to think about other people and you'll need to do what God instructs. These are two things you don't want to do when you make the choice to break one of God's rules.

Follow God. Chase after Him. Hold on. Be courageous. Stand strong.

Give me the wisdom to run from sinful choices, Father. Help me make decisions that You consider right.

VERY IMPORTANT PEOPLE

Whatever you say or do, . . .do it for the Lord and not for men.
COLOSSIANS 3:17, 23

★

People were not created to impress each other, but that's what people like to do. They want others to notice them and the things they do well so that they can be treated as if they are very important.

God really does want you to treat people as if they are very important not because of what they do but simply because God says people are important. People need to know someone is willing to pay attention to them. They need to know they're not alone.

God didn't only recognize you when you did something really cool. He noticed you before you were born. God doesn't need a reason to love you—He just does. You don't need a reason to love other people—just love them. And when you do, you're not doing it to make yourself famous. Instead, you're doing it because God asked you to, and you obeyed.

I follow You, Lord. I don't ask people to follow me unless it means we both follow You. Impressing people isn't as important as loving people. Help me keep this straight.

FIRST-TIME OBEDIENCE

Do all things without arguing and talking about how you wish you did not have to do them.
PHILIPPIANS 2:14

★

When you're asked to clean your room, do you have a good attitude about it, or do you sigh, stomp a bit, and make sure everyone knows you're not happy about your new assignment? That's the exact opposite of what God wants you to do.

You may not be interested in obeying, and you may want to tell everyone you meet that you're tired of doing what you're asked to do, but God's instructions say that is the wrong attitude to have.

Obey the first time and do it cheerfully. Leave your bad attitude behind, because no one likes to see that—not God, not your parents, and not even your friends.

You'll waste more time arguing and complaining than you will listening and obeying. God has already given instructions that say you should use time wisely on your quest with Him.

I don't want to whine or complain, Father, but sometimes I can't seem to help myself. Help me decide to obey You the first time I read or hear Your instructions. May I choose my attitude wisely.

YOUR BEST EXAMPLE

Work at being right with God. Live a God-like life.
1 Timothy 6:11

★

You're a boy who wants to be right with God. When you accept His gift of rescue, you begin your quest. This quest leads toward God, but it also leads away from everything that used to lead you to make choices that broke God's rules.

God wants you to live with nothing standing in the way of following. Breaking God's laws puts obstacles in the path of your quest. Being right with God, on the other hand, makes your path clear. Being right with God means doing what He says you should, not doing what He says you shouldn't, and then paying attention to what He wants you to do next.

You've discovered that God is your best example, and He wants you to do what He does. That includes things like loving and forgiving others, helping people, and making kindness a regular choice.

If you want to make the same kind of choices God makes, keep learning God's instructions.

Reading Your instructions has been easy, Lord.
But following them is sometimes hard.
Help me keep learning. Help me keep following.

THE PROBLEM WITH HATRED AND LIES

Put out of your life hate and lying.

1 PETER 2:1

God's instructions will always save you time; and if you trust God's wisdom, then you won't keep making choices that need forgiveness.

Today's instructions list two things you need to get rid of—hatred and lying. Don't invite either of them into your home.

Hatred and lies never give you enough time to love the truth. Your mind will want to think about how much you hate someone; or it will be wondering what lie you need to tell because you don't want other people to know the truth about something you've done. Choosing this path will draw you far away from God's quest.

In the end, you won't be thinking about God and how to obey Him if your mind and heart are infected with hatred and lies.

Some things just don't help me think straight, Father. Remove hatred and lies. I need better things to think about. Please give me new thoughts.

DON'T SETTLE, DON'T DOUBT

Live with love as Christ loved you.
EPHESIANS 5:2

★

Once you let God remove hatred and lies from your life, you'll need to replace those things with something else. If you don't, hatred and lies could invite themselves back into your life; and they might bring their friends greed, envy, and anger. Things get worse when they show up.

You are loved by God, and that love takes the place of hatred, lies, and all their friends. Things get better when love shows up. Love brings along other things like joy, peace, patience, and kindness. Let them in. They're good friends.

Make room for God by getting rid of everything you don't need. Give Him your life, and let Him show you how fulfilling it really can be. Don't settle for less. Don't doubt this new life is possible. After all, God is the One who made the promise, and God *always* keeps His promises.

Take what I don't need, Lord. Make room for Your great gifts. I need what I can't earn, and You give what I can't find anywhere else. Your love instructs me to look to You to help change me. Thank You for my new life!

VERY BIG GOD

Be quiet and know that I am God.
PSALM 46:10

★

So many things can cause stress in your life. You might worry about certain things or spend too much time and effort trying to take care of them. You might believe you have too much to do and no one to help—and the harder you try, the more difficult things become.

God's instructions tell you to knock it off. This is less of a statement that worry is pointless because God's got this; it's more of a statement that His power is so big that people everywhere will one day know how big He is. How can you know that? The second half of this verse says, "I will be honored among the nations. I will be honored in the earth."

You serve a big God who will be recognized by everyone. No one will need to open their mouth, ask questions, or wonder if it's true. When you feel stressed, remember the power of the One who walks beside you, and continue your quest with your very big God.

I never want to forget that You're God and You're my Father. Thanks for the reminder.

DON'T GIVE UP

"Hold on to what you have until I come."
REVELATION 2:25

★

God doesn't leave, turn His back, or abandon you. He has given you everything—from your very life to the food you eat. He has given you things to hope for and trust in. And for those times when life gets hard, He has given you some very important instructions. These instructions have to do with His gifts.

The Lord Jesus is coming back someday, so He said you should "hold on to what you have." And what you have are all the things God has given. There's no good reason to tell God you don't want His gifts. How could refusing His help benefit you?

It can be easy to give up when you have no hope. That's why you should never give up on the hope God has given you. He has promised you a future, so hold on to your trust in His promise.

You tell me to stand strong, Lord. You ask me to hold on, so I'm holding on to every promise. Give me patience in the waiting. Help me never to give up on Your gifts.

FULL OF JOY

Be full of joy always because you belong to the Lord. Again I say, be full of joy!
PHILIPPIANS 4:4

★

You don't know how things will turn out, but God does. He says they will turn out extraordinarily well, so you can "be full of joy!" God made you a family member, and you belong to Him, so "be full of joy!"

So many of God's instructions are practical. They help you know the best way to act, respond, and treat others. God made sure you would know that He takes care of everything and that nothing scares Him, beats Him, or takes Him by surprise. He is loving, merciful, and trustworthy.

This same God has a plan that includes you. He has a home in heaven waiting for you. He has forgiveness available to you right now. "Be full of joy!" Your quest isn't over, but the end will be amazing. "Again I say, be full of joy!"

There is never a moment when I can't find a reason to be full of joy, Father. Help me see Your blessings in the challenges I face, because every challenge is just another chance to see You work.

DON'T STOP THEM

Jesus said, "Let the little children come to Me. Do not stop them."
MATTHEW 19:14

★

Jesus gave today's instructions to adults. He wanted everyone to know that when children want to meet Him, they can.

You don't have to wait until you're a certain age. You don't have to pass a test. Your quest can start the moment you're rescued. He won't say, "I'm not sure you're ready yet." He won't say, "How about you come back next year when you're a little more grown up." He said that *now* is a good time to be rescued (see 2 Corinthians 6:2). So if now is a good time, there's no reason to wait.

You've read this book, so you know God has given a lot of instructions. There's no better time than when you're still a boy to tell God that you'll follow—and then actually start following His instructions on your journey home.

I'm happy to know there's no waiting to be close to You, Lord. Even as a boy, I can learn what You want and do what You ask. Thank You for inviting me to come to You!

WALK HIS WAY

"I am the Lord your God. So set yourselves apart, and be holy. For I am holy."
LEVITICUS 11:44

★

This quest that you're on is what you were created to do. Nothing else you do will be as important as following God and doing what He asks you to do. You're not to be one of the crowd walking toward Destruction City. You're on a narrow path, and God Himself is leading you. You're supposed to be different, and that's a good thing. God is set apart too. He is holy, and He calls you to be holy.

If the Lord is your God, then walk with Him, talk with Him, and allow Him to remind you of the instructions you may have forgotten. And don't hesitate to ask Him to introduce you to more instructions that will make your life quest beyond amazing.

God has given you instructions and the gifts and tools you need to carry them out. Use your gifts to complete your quest. You get to choose your next step. Will you walk His way?

I'm encouraged to continue my quest, Father. May I keep learning as You lead me today and every day of my life.